D0596772

ABORTION:
THE ULTIMATE EXPLOITATION OF WOMEN

ABORTION
THE ULTIMATE
EXPLOITATION OF WOMEN

Men Started It.

Men Oppress With It.

Men Can End It.

BRIAN E. FISHER

NEW YORK

ABORTION: THE ULTIMATE EXPLOITATION OF WOMEN
Men Started It. Men Oppress With It. Men Can End It.

© 2014 BRIAN E. FISHER. All rights reserved.

All rights reserved. No portion of this book may be reproduced, stored in a retrieval system, or transmitted in any form or by any means—electronic, mechanical, photocopy, recording, scanning, or other,—except for brief quotations in critical reviews or articles, without the prior written permission of the publisher.

Published in New York, New York, by Morgan James Publishing. Morgan James and The Entrepreneurial Publisher are trademarks of Morgan James, LLC.
www.MorganJamesPublishing.com

The Morgan James Speakers Group can bring authors to your live event. For more information or to book an event visit The Morgan James Speakers Group at www.TheMorganJamesSpeakersGroup.com.

Scripture taken from the New King James Version®. Copyright © 1982 by Thomas Nelson, Inc. Used by permission. All rights reserved.

FREE eBook edition for your existing eReader with purchase

———————————————
PRINT NAME ABOVE

For more information, instructions, restrictions, and to register your copy, go to www.bitlit.ca/readers/register or use your QR Reader to scan the barcode:

ISBN 978-1-61448-838-5 paperback
ISBN 978-1-61448-839-2 eBook
ISBN 978-1-61448-840-8 audio
ISBN 978-1-61448-841-5 hardcover
Library of Congress Control Number:
2013946702

Interior Design by:
Bonnie Bushman
bonnie@caboodlegraphics.com

In an effort to support local communities, raise awareness and funds, Morgan James Publishing donates a percentage of all book sales for the life of each book to Habitat for Humanity Peninsula and Greater Williamsburg.

Get involved today, visit www.MorganJamesBuilds.com.

Habitat for Humanity®
Peninsula and Greater Williamsburg Building Partner

CONTENTS

ACKNOWLEDGEMENTS

I am once again indebted to John Aman for his excellent and diligent work as researcher, editor, collaborator, criticizer, and encourager. This book is far better because of his passion and thoughtful input.

To Jessica, Caleb, and Zach, for their patience and understanding, as husband and father once again spent obscene amounts of time at home typing furiously behind a computer.

To the Directors, Advisory Board, and selfless donors of Online for Life, for their staunch support of our work.

To the OFL staff: Jeff Bradford, Tim Gerwing, Tommy Swanson, Sean Martin, Danielle Teel, Kari Buddenberg, Olga Figueroa, Barry Moerschell, and Ben Woodard, for insight, input, and hard work to print and distribute this book. And to the committed group of OFL volunteers, you have my deepest gratitude for your service.

To those contributors who courageously shared their abortion stories with me—thank you for your transparency and willingness to see others positively impacted by your experiences.

"YOUR BOOK TITLE MAKES NO SENSE"

ABORTION: THE ULTIMATE EXPLOITATION OF WOMEN.
That's a ridiculous title, isn't it?

Abortion doesn't exploit women—it empowers them. Abortion is a legal right for women that permits them to do whatever they want with their own bodies. Abortion has freed women from the bonds of male dominance and biological slavery. It has narrowed the gender gap and elevated the value and role of women in American society.

Abortion is choice, and choice is power.

**MEN STARTED IT. MEN OPPRESS WITH IT.
MEN CAN END IT.**
And what's this about men? They use abortion to oppress women? That's just crazy. Why would men promote abortion? They don't even have the legal right to influence the abortion decision. Socially, they aren't even really allowed to talk about it.

We are told that abortion has nothing to do with men. It is a huge step forward for women's rights.

There are three very good reasons why this should be true:

1. Abortion is legal in the United States, and that law empowers women. The landmark 1973 *Roe v. Wade* case effectively stripped men of any legal right to protect or terminate the life of a child in the womb. The Supreme Court decided the right to abort rests solely with women. It found that right in either the Fourteenth or the Ninth Amendment.[1] What it didn't find was any legal authority for a father to have a say about the fate of his offspring.

   In two subsequent abortion cases, the Court threw out a law requiring the husband's consent to his wife's abortion and another mandating that he be notified when his wife was on her way to an abortion facility. As the Court put it in the latter case, "[I]t cannot be claimed that the father's interest in the fetus' welfare is equal to the mother's protected liberty...."[2] So far as the Court is concerned, men have no rights whatsoever with respect to their progeny. The so-called right to privacy, as the Court said in *Roe*, "is broad enough to encompass a woman's decision whether or not to terminate her pregnancy"[3]—and to terminate the father's rights, as well.

2. Abortion is a surgical procedure that, for obvious reasons, only involves the female body. Because women are entrusted with providing sustenance and proper living conditions for a developing, *in utero* human being, any changes to that process must be carried out within the woman's body. Abortion is a surgical procedure that cannot be performed on men. Thus, men should not be able to dictate whether or not the surgical procedure is performed on women.

3. In America today, 40 percent of all births are out of wedlock.[4] With 24 percent of mothers raising kids without a father present,[5]

women are increasingly responsible not only for carrying a child during pregnancy—but for fully providing for that child once she is born.

We often speak of abortion in biological terms, constraining the conversation to life inside the womb. But the implications of raising a child after birth are very much a part of the abortion decision.

If the father of the child has abandoned the pregnant mother, she is now put in a very difficult position. She carries the emotional and physical weight of carrying the child before birth, and she now can anticipate a drastic change to her lifestyle, expenses, and social status after her child's birth.

The impact on lifestyle and finances are the two primary reasons women choose to abort in America today. A 2004 study conducted by researchers at the Guttmacher Institute—a pro-abortion organization—asked 1,209 women why they obtained abortions.

The reasons most frequently given: "having a baby would dramatically change my life" and "I can't afford a baby now" (cited by 74 and 73 percent, respectively).[6]

Since more and more men are leaving pregnant women without financial, emotional, or physical help, the decision to abort should rest with the gender responsible for the entire process. Author Kathleen McDonnell summarizes this view succinctly: "Women are the ones who bear children. Women are the ones, still, who are largely responsible for their care and nurturing. It is our bodies and our lives that are at issue, so the decisions must be ours as well."[7]

In a column responding to high school boys who petitioned her on behalf of the unborn child, *Cleveland Plain Dealer* writer Connie Schultz put it another way: "How do these boys figure that a woman's womb is any of their business? How do men, for that matter?"[8]

Indeed, how is it possible abortion is anything but an empowering decision for women? If the Supreme Court supports the woman's right to choose, biology mandates abortion only be performed on women, and women are increasingly being abandoned by men in the child-rearing process, why should men have any say at all?

For many men, it's just fine that they don't have the right to say anything. Their goal of using women to achieve their own selfish purposes has already been achieved. They now enjoy a new kind of freedom—a new kind of emancipation—because of a "woman's right to choose."

These "purposes" have very little to do with empowering women. In fact, man's relentless promotion of abortion exploits women in the most personal, debilitating, and disrespectful way. It is yet another tool to persecute and diminish women, pushing them farther away from gender equality. In the process, men are doing enormous damage to the physical and emotional well-being of millions of American women and their families.

And men walk away from the damage with no responsibility or accountability. In fact, we are able to give the same passive rationalization we've been giving for millennia: "It's her fault. It's her responsibility. Not mine."

How is it, then, that our culture celebrates abortion as a woman's choice? It's her body; it's her life. If men are behind the abortion issue, why is it that women are taking full responsibility for the choice and its consequences?

The answer is simple: That's exactly what pro-abortion men want our culture to think.

Early feminists were passionately against abortion, understanding that abortion exploited and harmed women.

In fact, I didn't invent the book title, "The Ultimate Exploitation of Women." The original architect of the Equal Rights Amendment coined the phrase to describe abortion and its impact on females. Her name was Alice Paul, and she was a feminist.

But time, effective marketing and messaging, and money changed the culture.

And while men achieve their social and personal goals, women are victimized, yet celebrate their own exploitation and call it a right. Our culture bought the lie, and now millions of women celebrate their own degradation.

Women aren't the only victims of abortion. There are many thousands of men who, today, continue to mourn the loss of children they had no legal right to protect. And there are untold family members of both genders who have been deeply wounded by abortion.

And, of course, there are well over 55 million human beings of both genders who have lost their lives to abortion—the most innocent victims of all.

If you are a post-abortive woman who regrets having an abortion, it's important for you to know that I (and thousands of others) do not hold you in contempt or judge you. In fact, mercy, compassion, and grace are extended to you, and I hope you have found it or are on your way to doing so.

If you are a post-abortive man with regrets, know that I've spent time with men who lost children to abortion and are now deeply hurt because of it. In many cases it was your pressure, passivity, or pocketbook that caused it. In some cases, you desperately wanted to keep your child and had no legal right to do so. Either way, you lost. There is hope and healing for you, also, and I pray you find it.

If you are a post-abortive woman who does not regret the abortion decision and continues to favor abortion rights, there is no contempt or judgment for you. Abortion is legal, and you exercised your legal right to abort. I urge you, though, to confront the reality of the after effects of abortion and its horrific impact on society and your gender. And I will challenge your premise that abortion furthers gender equality. It does not. You are being manipulated in ways that are terribly unfair and unjust to women.

If you are a man who favors abortion (post-abortive or not), I challenge you to read this book and consider its facts. My hope is you will at least take responsibility for your role and acknowledge the degrading impact abortion has on women, men, the family, and society. Your active or passive promotion of abortion is destroying the fabric of what makes America great. This isn't opinion. It is fact.

And for those men who claim they support life and true gender equality, I say this: Abortion will not be ended in America until you do something. As someone who sat on the sidelines for years, doing nothing to protect women and the unborn from abortion, I urge you to read this book and take action. I'll give you some productive recommendations on what to do in the last chapter.

Just as abortion was wrought on America by men, it will only be ended in America when men stand beside women, as equals, to cooperatively rid America of the death and suffering.

Don't just sit there and say you affirm life. Saying you affirm life, but doing nothing, makes you irrelevant. Don't be that guy.

ONE HOUSEKEEPING NOTE

I do not use the term "pro-choice" in this book unless it is a quotation. I use the term "pro-abortion" or "abortion proponent." This is not because I am attempting to upset those who favor abortion. It is because the term "pro-choice" is misleading and incorrect.

There is a widely-held belief that one can be pro-choice and not pro-abortion. This means that a person supports the right to choose abortion but generally wishes abortion wouldn't happen.

To be "pro-choice" means one is in favor of having options or choices. To be "pro-abortion" means one is in favor of the legality and practice of abortion.

I am as pro-choice as it gets. I am in favor of women having a myriad of options: where to go to college, what career to pursue, whether or not she wants to get married, who she marries, who to vote for, whether or not she wants to run a business, what she wants to do with her free time, whether or not to enter politics, etc.

However, I do not believe that any person, whether male or female, should have the option to take the life of another innocent human being.

The term "pro-choice" was invented in the mid-1970s to avoid using the term "pro-abortion," a designation which "in the pre-*Roe* years had served as the standard label for a person in favor of legalization [of abortion]."[9] Former abortionist Bernard Nathanson, a founding member of NARAL (National Association for the Repeal of Abortion Laws), the group that led efforts to legalize abortion, called "pro-choice" a "Madison Avenue euphemism."[10]

The goal of this effort by abortion activists to "remake the vocabulary with which Americans talked about abortion," as abortion historian Cynthia Gorney described it,[11] was to take attention off the abortion procedure and loss of life, and instead make the issue about women's rights.

But to be in favor of the choice to take a life is to be in support of the practice of doing so. One could argue that to be offered the choice to abort is not the same as actually aborting. But one's permission to do something is condoning and, therefore, supporting that practice.

The opposite of pro-life is not pro-choice; it's pro-abortion—in favor of the practice of abortion.

My goal in writing this book is to shed light on the victimization of women, showing that the female gender is under attack in America. While I am life affirming, I am also a proponent of true equal rights for both genders, and that is the focus of this book.

Ending abortion in America would not just benefit the millions of children who lose their lives each year. It would be an enormous step forward for women in their appropriate quest for equal rights and equal protection. And, if men would be so convicted, ending the practice would be a step forward in their quest to live out their appropriate roles as selfless partners, serving alongside women for their shared and mutual good.

Brian Fisher

CHAPTER 1

JUST A WOMEN'S ISSUE?

There is no topic as heated, controversial, and emotional in America today as abortion. It seems everyone has an opinion on it, and expressing those opinions is likely to start a lively, impassioned debate.

In many cases, though, we don't talk about it. Abortion has entered the cultural realm of "religion" and "politics"—subjects we don't talk about in the company of family, coworkers, and strangers. It's too awkward, too personal, too heavy, and will likely invite conflict we want to avoid.

I've tested the premise that people don't like to talk about abortion, and the anecdotal results are sometimes humorous, sometimes sad, sometimes frustrating.

The conversation may go like this: "So, Brian, what do you do for a living?" "I work to rescue mothers, fathers, and babies from abortion."

Once in awhile, someone will respond with great enthusiasm, anxious to hear about that work.

Too often, the person will look aside. I have learned what that means. They are post-abortive and have just been reminded of it. Sometimes they will tell me their story, but most of the time they quickly change the conversation. I suspect most post-abortive people expect me to be judgmental and think ill of them. That's not the case, as I have too often

1

seen the intense pain and shame abortion brings. Abortion creates all sorts of victims.

Sometimes a person will immediately change the subject and go to great lengths to make sure we don't come back around to that subject. That generally means someone is highly in favor of abortion and doesn't want to get into a discussion about it.

It is rare that someone actually engages in a conversation about abortion in America. Abortion has now been relegated to the dustbin of topics we shouldn't talk about.

Yet abortion has saturated our culture and pervades just about every area of our lives. Statistics suggest every family in America has been touched by abortion in some way or other.

ABORTION IMPACTS EVERYONE

Consider just a few brief facts:

- Abortion is one of the most common surgical procedures in the U.S.
- It is the leading cause of death (heart disease kills 600,000 annually while 1.2 million pre-born children die each year from abortion).[12]
- Over 55 million Americans have lost their lives to abortion since 1973.
- 3 in ten women in America are post-abortive by the time they are 45.[13] This implies that around 30 percent of men are also post-abortive. (Post-abortive means, if you are a woman, you've had an abortion. If you are a man, you are the father of an aborted child.)
- Abortion is an enormous industry, generating more than $800 million[14] each year for abortion doctors, facilities, and providers. Black market industries exist around the business of abortion.[15]
- Virtually every major city in America has at least one abortion clinic. Most large cities have several.

- Pharmaceutical abortions (abortion using a pill such as RU-486) continue to rise in popularity.
- There are hundreds of nonprofit organizations attempting to reduce or eliminate abortion, and there are numerous such organizations promoting it. There is no shortage of ink spilled over the abortion issue online, in magazines, and in the papers. It is a constant topic on TV, whether in our pop culture (*16 and Pregnant*) or in the news.

Our political candidates declare a formal position on the topic before every election.

Over the past 40 years, abortion has become part of our families, part of our communities, and part of our culture.

If abortion is so pervasive and common, can it really just be a woman's issue?

The mainstream media and pro-abortion organizations continue to assert as much. Planned Parenthood, the largest abortion provider in the United States, celebrated the 40th Anniversary of *Roe v. Wade* by stating, "That's 40 years of protecting every woman's fundamental right to make her own personal medical decisions."

Since *Roe v. Wade* effectively supports that assertion, it's no surprise that many men and women fully support it, especially in politics and entertainment:

"I remain committed to protecting a woman's right to choose and this fundamental constitutional right.... [W]e must also continue our efforts to ensure that our daughters have the same rights, freedoms, and opportunities as our sons to fulfill their dreams."

—President Barack Obama[16]

"Being pro-choice is trusting the individual to make the right decision for herself and her family, and not entrusting that decision to anyone wearing the authority of government in any regard."

—Hillary Clinton[17]

"Reproductive choice is a fundamental human right and we can never take it for granted. On this issue, you're either with us or against us."

—New York Mayor Michael Bloomberg[18]

"The people who say that we shouldn't have the right to choose, that the government should interfere with our womb, are not people who believe in helping mothers who are poor or psychologically or emotionally unfit or unable to have children...."

—Jane Fonda[19]

"Can small-minded idiot blokes stop telling women whether or not they're entitled to abortions please?"

—Lily Allen[20]

"We are deeply disturbed by…the growing movement to limit women's reproductive rights. And as Mother's Day approaches, we join Planned Parenthood in their fight to protect women…across the country."[21]

—Gwyneth Paltrow and Blythe Danner

"I support the Supreme Court decision that says an abortion is a woman's decision, very difficult decision, to be made privately in conjunction with her religious beliefs, her doctor, her responsibility to her family—and the government is completely inappropriate in that decision."

—Susan Sarandon[22]

ABORTION IMPACTS MEN

But is abortion really just about females? Is it just about their bodies, their choices, and their rights? Or is there something else going on beneath the surface?

Obviously, the act of abortion impacts both genders. Both males and females lose their lives in the womb.

Though there are numerous arguments about when an unborn child is a person or should have rights, there is no longer any rational disagreement about when human life begins. Human life begins at conception. A unique, completely distinct human being is wonderfully created at conception. She has all of the genetic material she needs to continue to mature through the phases of pregnancy, birth, and beyond.

The purpose of this book is not to argue the topic of "personhood" (which is dealt with fairly by Robert George and Christopher Tollefsen in their book, *Embryo: A Defense of Human Life*). The process of assigning value to a human life at some point beyond conception is subjective and variable. Science has proven that life begins at conception—and that life is a member of the species *Homo sapiens*, a human being.

Thus abortion is, by definition, the willful termination of a human life. Very few abortion proponents today argue otherwise—mainly because the facts of life are conclusive.

So it stands to reason that around half of the 55 million babies aborted in America over the last 40 years were male. Abortion most certainly impacts the male gender.

Ironically, though males are aborted, the procedure disproportionately culls unborn females through sex-selection abortions. Some 200 million girls worldwide are missing[23] due to this practice, which takes place even in the U.S.[24]

However, not every human being who is aborted dies. There are numerous cases of "abortion survivors," human beings who were aborted, didn't die, and were then born. Many of those survivors are male.

Take Josiah Presley, for instance. Josiah was aborted by his mother in South Korea but survived. He was eventually adopted by parents in the U.S. and is a perfectly normal young man (save his left arm, which was presumably damaged in the abortion attempt).

Other men are alive today because their mothers, though encouraged to abort, chose, instead, to carry their babies. Singer, entertainer, and TV personality Nick Cannon and NFL quarterback Tim Tebow are both examples of grown men saved from potential death in the womb by their own mothers.

Other men were saved from abortion even though their mothers were raped. Activist and media expert Ryan Bomberger is alive today because his mother, who was raped, chose to carry Ryan and place him for adoption.

All of these men have strong opinions about abortion, and their existence proves men have been profoundly influenced by it.

Should these men be silenced because of the impact abortion has had on them personally? Should men be silent when tens of millions of male humans have perished in the womb?

MARS AND VENUS ACTUALLY AGREE

Much is made in the media about abortion as a dividing line between men and women. But the so-called "gender gap" on abortion—based on the idea that this is a women's issue—doesn't exist. Men and women think alike on abortion. A recent Pew Poll found "no gender gap in opinions about *Roe v. Wade*: Nearly identical percentages of women (64 percent) and men (63 percent) oppose reversing the decision."[25]

The real split over abortion falls along religious lines. Fifty percent of people who attend religious services at least weekly want *Roe* overturned, while just 17 percent of those who attend worship less than weekly favor *Roe's* reversal.

"YOU CAN SPEAK YOUR MIND ...
AS LONG AS WE AGREE"

Men are welcomed to take a position favoring abortion. They are even welcomed to take a neutral, passive stance. But they are not welcomed to take a public stance for life. If they do, they are derided and accused of being anti-woman, anti-reproductive rights, and traditionalist. Sometimes just being a man makes you suspect to pro-abortion feminists, which is why attorney and activist Florynce Kennedy once cracked, "If men could get pregnant, abortion would be a sacrament."

The educational organization I work for, Online for Life, recently released an iPhone app that allows people to pray for families considering abortion. One woman reviewed the app and wrote, "I have aborted several babies from my uterus. When did they (men at Online for Life) get vaginas? Oh wait. They didn't. Good luck with this bologna."

Another wrote, "Hey Brian, how completely self-righteous of you to proclaim you know what's best for anyone but yourself. Especially in the cases of pregnant women, considering you'll never experience pregnancy and don't know their circumstances. This app is crazy town. Mind your own business."

The point is this: because the abortion procedure is performed on a woman's body, men have no right to opine or intrude.

What abortion defenders say, in effect, is "You can't get pregnant, so leave the abortion issue to women," as life-affirming debater Scott Klusendorf points out. He calls it the "I don't like you" objection. The fact is, arguments don't have genders. They're either true or false, regardless of whether they are made by a man or a woman.

If, as some have argued, the qualification for addressing the abortion issue is the ability to bear children, then *Roe* itself is thrown into question, and all the men who legalized abortion and work in the abortion advocacy business ought to look for work elsewhere. Seven of the nine men on the Supreme Court voted for the legalization of abortion. Should their votes not have counted because they didn't have uteruses? What about the numerous men who work for Planned Parenthood, the ACLU, and other pro-abortion organizations? Should their voices be counted?

In fact, they are heard. The only voices not allowed to speak are those of men who are not in favor of abortion. As Klusendorf points out, the argument ought to be restated, "No man can speak on abortion unless he agrees with us."[26]

Prostate cancer kills thousands of men each year. Men care very much about prostate cancer, and they should have access to resources in order to be properly educated, so they can avoid getting it. Does that mean that women, who don't have male organs, have no right to talk about prostate cancer? Or do both genders agree that prostate cancer kills men?

Facts are facts. A person's gender does not change those facts or reduce one's right to discuss them.

MEN AS VICTIMS

We are inclined to accept that women should be the only gender with an opinion, right, and authority to choose abortion. After all, they are the ones who experience pregnancy, the abortion itself, and its after effects.

Yet more and more evidence suggests that men are also victims of abortion.

Dr. Keith Ablow, a psychiatrist, says he has "listened to dozens of men express lingering, sometimes intense, pain over abortions that proceeded either without their consent, or without them having spoken up about their desires to bring their children to term and parent them."[27]

Shawn Carney, the campaign director of 40 Days for Life, witnessed the anguish of a Korean man unable to prevent his wife from aborting their child. The man begrudgingly drove his wife to an abortion facility in Texas and waited in their parked car with their two young children while his wife went in for her abortion. Carney observed all this while standing outside the clinic fence. After a while, the man left his car and approached Carney with a gut-wrenching appeal. Carney writes:

> ... he was yelling over and over: "I love children! I love children! Please go get her!" I moved closer to the fence, and he explained to me that he didn't want the abortion. "Please, go get her!" he screamed. "Can't you do something? I love children!" He pointed desperately to his other two kids in the minivan. "I don't want her abortion. Can't you go in and do something?"

Carney was powerless to help—except to pray—and, ultimately, the man who had been begging Carney to act started to weep in his despair. Unable to stop the death of his own child, he released his grip on the bars of the fence separating the two men and "slid to the ground, his shoulders slumped and heaving."[28]

Another post-abortive male, Phil McCombs, a journalist at *The Washington Post*, wrote a public confession, laced with guilt and regret, of the abortion of his child. "I feel like a murderer," McCombs wrote, telling readers that he made sure he was out of town when his partner got the abortion. "I was not by her side to support her. I turned my face away. My behavior was in all respects craven, immoral." The child, who he came to believe was a boy, "would have inconvenienced me. I'd had my fun. He didn't fit into my plans.... His name, which is carved on my heart, was Thomas," he wrote. "I still grieve for little Thomas. It is an ocean of grief."[29]

My dear friend and co-worker, Jeff Bradford, knows the pain of abortion first hand:

> I hid and suppressed the realization that the only reason our oldest daughter was not alive today was due to my own cowardice. I went to my wedding, pretending to be an upright, moral young man with my bride dressed all in white. She was beautiful, and we looked great on the outside. No one could see the brokenness we were both hiding so well. We had aborted our first child just a few months before.
>
> For 15 years, I was too ashamed to tell anyone what I had done, except my best friend. My wife and I never talked about it, we did not grieve together, and we hid it deep in the recesses of our minds. Our marriage began to unravel, and through extensive counseling, we realized how much of our struggle had come down to the decision to end the life of our first child. We began to deal with our own shame and guilt. We realized the extent of the mental and emotional trauma it had caused. There were many levels—resentment, a lack of forgiveness, feelings of abandonment—all revealed as we dealt with the reality of this decision many years earlier.
>
> Now, as a father of four beautiful children, and through God's grace, my wife and I are healing and have been married 20 years. However, there is not a day that goes by that I don't regret my decision. After all, any good father would jump in front of a train to save the life of his child. The life of our first daughter, Sara, should not have been any different.

Not every story has a sad ending, though some are more ironic than others.

While we often associate abortion with a single mother and a deadbeat father, abortion frequently impacts married couples who already have kids.

While we may feel disdain for fathers who leave their pregnant partners to pursue the next woman, do we also feel disdain for married men who want to protect their own unborn children—but have no legal right to do so?

Do we think that a father who has provided a stable, secure home for his family should have no say in the welfare of his own unborn child?

The day after Christmas a woman, we'll call her Sarah, telephoned a local, life-affirming center (a local, community-based organization designed to educate families about pregnancy and options other than abortion). She had already taken two home pregnancy tests—both positive. She had decided to abort her baby. After she had a few questions answered, the woman said she was going to call a few other clinics. The center asked permission to follow up with her in a few days, and she agreed.

Sarah called back the next day on her own, asking if she could come in for an ultrasound. She had called abortion clinics, discovered she couldn't get an abortion appointment in her own city for a few weeks, and was preparing to go out of state so she could get the procedure done sooner. Because she needed to verify the pregnancy with an ultrasound before the abortion, she agreed to come into the life-affirming center.

Sarah came in that day with her husband, Paul. While she was having her ultrasound, the staff spoke with him.

"I don't want her to get the abortion. I don't like abortion and don't understand why she doesn't want the child," Paul said.

Sarah's reasons were simple. The couple already had a little girl, and she didn't want another baby. She was going to school to get her degree, and another child would make that education very difficult to attain. She wasn't mentally or emotionally ready to be a new mom again.

The center gave her the ultrasound and talked to her about pregnancy, the child, and her options.

The couple left. Paul wanted to have the child; Sarah was now unsure if she wanted to abort.

Several days later, the center called Paul to follow up. Paul was overjoyed to report that Sarah had changed her mind, and they were going to carry and parent their child.

"I can't thank you enough for talking to her," he said. "I so appreciate your help."

Here's the twist: Paul is a policeman. His job is to protect people, even if it means putting himself in harm's way. Yet he had no legal or cultural authority to protect his own unborn child, whom he desperately wanted to live.

The moment his child was born, Paul would have legal rights as a father to do everything possible to protect and provide for his child. And his job requires him to do that for complete strangers every day. Yet, though he wanted his own child to live, he was helpless to protect the baby while she was growing in her mother's womb.

These are just a few examples of the devastating impact abortion has on men—both those who support women in their abortions and those forced to stand and watch while their girlfriends or wives abort their children against their will. The powerlessness imposed on men by the law goes against our very nature as protectors and defenders.

So is abortion just a women's issue? Do the millions of males lost to abortion have a voice? Do post-abortive men, who now often suffer in silence, have a voice? Do those men who want to keep their children, but are powerless to stop abortions, have a voice?

Making men sit on the sidelines because it's a "women's issue" conveniently assumes, but does not prove, that the unborn are not members of the human race with the same dignity and right to live as the rest of us. If that unstated assumption is exposed and answered by the facts of science, we're left with a discussion about whether it's right or wrong to kill innocent, helpless, vulnerable humans—male and female—at early stages of their development. That's a human rights debate—one in which women have no monopoly.

But, of course, abortion is legal, so why are we discussing this at all? After all, if the law says it's okay, that means it is right and good. Right?

CHAPTER 2

Our Laws are Always Right... Right?

Including abortion in the long list of ways men exploit women may be utterly disagreeable and distasteful to you. Our culture has long accepted that abortion is a woman's right, both socially and legally. How can 40 years of law and decades of social education be wrong? How can something that is clearly a woman's right actually be a way of discriminating against women?

You may well argue that abortion is an obvious benefit to women and society. After all, tens of millions of women and men have taken advantage of its availability. If it is legal, how can it be bad for women and families?

Can a right actually be a form of bondage? Can a legal right be wrong?

Indeed, both can be true. Within the last two centuries, another American practice was both legal and socially accepted—but was actually a form of discrimination and bondage.

DRED SCOTT – GOOD LAW?

Much ink has already been spilt on comparisons between the African slave trade and abortion. My purpose is not to rewrite it—but to illustrate that law and social norms do not immediately validate the claim that a practice promotes equality or is for the betterment of society.

Slavery existed for 250 years in America and defined away the humanity and legal status of a whole class of human beings. It, too, had the U.S. Supreme Court's stamp of approval. U.S. Supreme Court Chief Justice Roger B. Taney determined, in the 1857 *Dred Scott* case, that African Americans were "regarded as beings of an inferior order, and altogether unfit to associate with the white race, either in social or political relations, and so far unfit that they had no rights which the white man was bound to respect."[30]

We cringe at the odious racism in Chief Justice Taney's ruling, but the verbiage and tone of that case are strikingly similar to the tone of *Roe v. Wade*, the case that made abortion legal in the U.S. The decision diminishes the unborn, referring to the unborn child as "potential life," and says "meaningful life" may arise later in pregnancy. *Roe* author Justice Harry Blackmun cites early English common law for this view that it is only later in pregnancy when the "fetus became 'formed' or recognizably human, or … when a 'person' came into being…."[31]

In an eerie echo of *Dred Scott*, *Roe* denied legal protection to the unborn because, as the Court concluded, "[T]he word 'person,' as used in the Fourteenth Amendment, does not include the unborn."[32] The Fourteenth Amendment was adopted in 1868 and declares, "No State shall … deprive any person of life, liberty, or property, without due process of law; nor deny to any person within its jurisdiction the equal protection of the laws."

If Justice Blackmun, the author of *Roe*, had been willing to recognize the personhood of the unborn (and if they're not "persons," what are they?), he would have had to rule the other way, as he admitted: "If this suggestion of personhood [for the unborn child] is established … the fetus' right to life would then be guaranteed specifically by the [Fourteenth] Amendment."[33]

And having determined that the unborn are not persons under the Fourteenth Amendment, the Court really didn't have to opine on when life begins. Blackmun punted, claiming that since "those trained in the respective disciplines of medicine, philosophy, and theology are unable to arrive at any consensus [about when life begins], the judiciary, at this point in the development of man's knowledge, is not in a position to speculate as to the answer."[34]

When life begins is no deep conundrum at all. And it's not a theological or philosophical question. We're not asking Who is the author of life or what rules He has ordained for the living. Nor are we asking what the value or purpose of life is. When we ask when life begins, we're asking a scientific question that science can answer. And it has done so definitively. Life begins at conception, i.e., fertilization. One popular embryology textbook describes it this way:

> ... human development begins at fertilization when a male gamete or sperm (spermatozoon) unites with a female gamete or oocyte (ovum) to form a single cell—a zygote. This highly specialized totipotent cell marked the beginning of each of us as a unique individual.[35]

But *Roe* does not cite science. It simply says the unborn are not persons in the eyes of the law, just as African-American slaves were not persons under the *Dred Scott* decision. As horrific as slavery was, the "liberty" granted in *Roe* is much worse, since it grants a freedom not merely to own and enslave other humans—but to use deadly force against weak and vulnerable members of the human family.

In other words, *Roe* denies rights to the unborn on the basis of personhood, but it doesn't even bother to determine when life actually begins.

Slavery was legal because the law determined African Americans were not persons.

Abortion is legal because the law determined pre-born humans are not persons.

Was slavery legal? Yes. Was it good? No.

Is abortion legal? Yes. Is it good?

The fact that abortion is legal, freely practiced, and socially acceptable does not mean it is good for women. It just means it is legal, freely practiced, and socially acceptable.

Slavery met the same criteria, though today we consider slavery to be reprehensible, noting that slavery is inherently discriminatory towards slaves. And, if you think about it, abortion is equally discriminatory against a whole class of human beings—those who are small, dependent, voiceless, and in a location where we can't see them without medical assistance.

IS SHE A PERSON OR NOT?

Then there are those bizarre legal circumstances that call the legality of abortion into question altogether.

On April 13, 2003, the body of a late-term male fetus washed up on the shore of San Francisco Bay. One day later, the partial body of his mother washed up a mile or so away.

Though the exact cause of death was never determined, it was concluded that the mother, Laci Peterson, was murdered by her husband, Scott.

Scott was charged and convicted of first-degree murder in the death of his wife.

He was also charged with second-degree murder in the death of his unborn son, Conner.

The situation is tragic, sad—and incredibly ironic. Scott was charged with second-degree murder in the death of his unborn son yet, in many states, Laci could have aborted the same child, and it would have been perfectly legal.

So Conner's death was illegal because his dad caused it, but it would have been perfectly legal if his mom had caused it.

This high-profile crime led to a federal law that defies logic—the Unborn Victims of Violence Act.

Signed into law in 2004 by President George W. Bush, "Laci and Conner's Law" recognizes a child *in utero* as a legal victim if he or she is injured or killed during the act of over 60 federal crimes of violence. The law defines the unborn child as a member of the species *Homo sapiens*, at any stage of development, who is carried in the mother's womb.

The law has a specific exemption for abortion that didn't satisfy its critics. Senator John Kerry voted against the bill, remarking, "I have serious concerns about this legislation because the law cannot simultaneously provide that a fetus is a human being and protect the right of the mother to choose to terminate her pregnancy."[36]

Senator Kerry made a valid point. One law protects the unborn child at any stage of development from acts of violence, yet another law denies the same protection to the same child. Apparently the value and status of the child is determined by who does the act of violence—not the child itself. One law makes it clear that the unborn child is a member of the human race, while the other isn't sure but allows for the willful termination of the life anyhow.

Both Laci and Conner's Law and *Roe v. Wade* are legal—while completely paradoxical. And, in the worst form of discrimination, the value of the human life in the womb is determined, legally, by whoever opts to take that life.

So we must, therefore, look at abortion through a different lens for two reasons. Current U.S. law regarding the status of the unborn is in conflict with itself, and just because something is legal doesn't make it right or good.

The fact that we say abortion is about women's rights does not mean it advances gender equality.

Just as it is vital to remind ourselves about the racial and selfish reasons behind slavery, we must also peer behind the curtain to understand the rationale behind the legality of abortion.

So, yes, abortion is legal. But that doesn't mean it is automatically good for women, families, and society as a whole.

Men Started It

CHAPTER 3

A LONG HISTORY OF MEN BEHAVING BADLY

While there are millions of examples of wise, kind, gentle, and respectful men in history, there are also far too many examples of men who took it upon themselves to treat women as property.

Men often actively seek to use women to their own ends. And sometimes men accomplish the same ends by doing nothing.

ANCIENT MEN BEHAVING BADLY

The most famous example of a man standing by while his wife hurt herself happened in an ancient and beautiful garden. Though Adam was with his perfect wife, Eve, in the Garden of Eden when she fatefully took a bite of the forbidden fruit, he still managed to blame God when he went right along with her disobedience.

When God inquired what had happened, Adam replied, "The woman whom You gave to be with me, she gave me of the tree, and I ate" (Genesis 3:12). Not only did Adam sit by when Eve was tempted to disobey, he refused to take responsibility for not protecting his own wife.

After Adam and Eve were cast out of the garden, things went downhill for women in general. Most ancient civilizations viewed women as slaves and property.

In ancient Greece, women had little to no freedom. Historian and biographer Plutarch remarked that women were to be kept "under lock and key." In a play by Aristophanes, the female character, Calonice, says, "We women can't go out just when we like. We have to wait upon our men."[37]

Sociologist Alvin J. Schmidt gives a troubling overview of the way women were treated in ancient Greece. Schmidt, author of *How Christianity Changed the World*, details the ways in which the average woman had the social status of a slave:

- She had no legal ability to divorce her husband.
- Girls were not allowed to attend school and receive an education,
- Women were not allowed to speak in public.
- Legally, women were deemed to be inferior to men.
- Infanticide was common, and the babies killed were overwhelmingly female.

Ancient Rome treated women much the same. At the time of Christ, according to Schmidt, women had "none of the rights and privileges that men enjoyed."

- Husbands had absolute control of wives and their possessions. Women owned nothing.
- Wives could not divorce their husbands.
- Women could not inherit property.
- The law gave a husband the right to physically punish his wife. That punishment could include death.
- Women were not allowed to speak in public.[38]

The relative worth of girls in the ancient world is revealed in this astonishing first century letter from a Roman man to his pregnant wife:

I send you my warmest greetings. I want you to know that we are still in Alexandria. And please don't worry.... If you have the baby before I return, if it is a boy, let it live; if it is a girl expose it....[39]

Sexually, women were tools for men's pleasure. Church historian Philip Schaff remarks, "The virtue of chastity, in our Christian sense, was almost unknown among the heathens. Woman was essentially a slave of man's lower passions."[40]

Plutarch notes that child brides were common, with girls being married off as young as 12. These girls had no options, no choices, and no voice about who they married.

Women were also held in low regard in first century Jewish culture. The Talmud, for example, contains this observation: "The world cannot exist without males and without females—happy is he whose children are males, and woe to him whose children are females."[41] The testimony of women was regarded as suspect or not accepted. As first century Jewish historian Josephus wrote, "But let not the testimony of women be admitted, on account of the levity and boldness of their sex...."[42]

Until Christianity worked to stop the practice in Hindu India, the burning of widows was a common occurrence. It was considered the duty of a good wife to sacrifice herself on her husband's funeral pyre. According to a Hindu saying, "If her husband is happy, she should be happy; if he is sad, she should be sad; and if he is dead, she should also die."[43] This duty was forcibly imposed on willing and unwilling widows. The practice was also common in pre-Christian Scandinavia, China, New Zealand, and among some American Indians, prior to Columbus' arrival.[44]

In China, binding women's feet was common practice for centuries. The process, involving painfully and tightly wrapping young girls' feet to prevent normal growth, often resulted in lifelong disability, pain, and lack of mobility for the women. Why did Chinese men institute and promote foot binding? Because they found women with a limited gait more attractive.[45]

Though it can be argued that men have found numerous ways to mistreat, torture, and abuse other men (slavery, for instance), there are no national examples of women binding men's feet, forcing them to wear certain articles of clothing, using them as property for their own pleasure, or having the legal right to kill their husbands.

In the interaction of genders across world history, if inequality and abuse was present, it was always women suffering at the hands of men.

Female inequality, exploitation, and maltreatment are not limited to ancient times in other cultures. America, too, has a long history of female inequality.

AMERICAN MEN BEHAVING BADLY

Not that women in early America experienced anything like the oppression and mistreatment of women in the ancient world. Women in America have historically enjoyed far more freedom than in any other culture. In *Democracy in America*, Alexis de Tocqueville's epic survey of 1830s America, the author remarks, "[W]omen of the United States are confined within the narrow circle of domestic life, and their situation is in some respects one of extreme dependence." At the same time, "I have nowhere seen women occupying a loftier position."[46]

Women in 19th century America did not have equal rights with men. They did not have the right to vote, lost property rights when they married, and had few options for divorce or employment outside the home. As the "Declaration of Sentiments," a feminist document signed at the 1856 Seneca Falls Convention, put it, speaking of the male-dominant society at the time:

- He has never permitted her to exercise her inalienable right to the elective franchise.
- He has compelled her to submit to laws, in the formation of which she had no voice.
- He has withheld from her rights which are given to the most ignorant and degraded men—both natives and foreigners.
- Having deprived her of this first right of a citizen, the elective franchise, thereby leaving her without representation in the halls of legislation, he has oppressed her on all sides.[47]

It was not until 1920 that American women won the right to vote with the passage of the 19th Amendment. The first 33 American Presidents were men elected by men (though some states permitted women to vote in 1916).

And while America has arguably been the most progressive country in moving towards equal rights for women, many parts of the world are still in the dark ages of gender inequality.

MODERN MEN BEHAVING BADLY

I recently had lunch with a new friend who works in the medical field in the African country of Uganda. I asked him about the culture, the medical facilities, and the presence of abortion. My friend, Emma (a man's name in his country), told me abortion is illegal in Uganda, though widely practiced. When I asked him how that could be, he replied, "The women do the work. They bear the children, raise the children, and also have to work to provide for their families. So they get abortions because they have no money and no help around the home."

"What do the men do?" I asked.

"Nothing. They sit around all day. They drink and smoke."

"They do nothing?" I inquired with surprise.

"Nothing. Lazy. They think women should do everything."

This chauvinistic philosophy and practice is not limited to Uganda. It is widely reported in numerous African countries.

In the Middle East, Sharia law is used in many Islamic nations to impose strict and restrictive laws on women. In Saudi Arabia, the birthplace of Islam, the law places severe limitations on women. Under Saudi law and custom, for example, women

- are not allowed to go out without male accompaniment,
- are not allowed to drive,
- are not allowed to vote, and
- must, in most cases, wear a head covering, a full black cloak, and a face veil when out in public.

"Saudi society is based on enslavement—the enslavement of women to men and of society to the state," Wajiha Al-Huweidar, a Saudi Arabian woman and activist for women's rights, said on Al-Hurra TV on January 13, 2008. "People still do not make their own decisions," she said, "but it is the women of Saudi Arabia who have been denied everything. The Saudi woman still lives the life of a slave girl."[48]

Other Islamic nations, including Egypt, impose strict regulations on female movement and lifestyle. Egyptian-born Noni Darwish noted the practical implications of such restrictions. In her book, *Cruel and Usual Punishment*, which reveals the harsh impact of Sharia law on women, Darwish writes, "For the first thirty years of my life, I lived as a virtual slave. I was a bird in a cage: a second-class citizen who had to watch what I said even to my close friends."[49]

Darwish, born in 1949, writes, "During my years in Egypt, the vast majority of Muslim women lived in cramped apartments or unhealthy little mud huts, spending their entire lives working hard under the severe Egyptian sun."

There are numerous examples of Muslim women publicly executed because they were raped or suspected of adultery. In Bangladesh, a 14-year-old girl collapsed and died after receiving 70 lashes. Her punishment came after an older male cousin allegedly attacked, gagged, and raped her. A local imam said she was guilty of adultery and sentenced her to a public whipping of 100 lashes. CNN reported that her parents "watched as the whip broke the skin of their youngest child and she fell unconscious to the ground."[50]

The brutality is even more horrific in Iran. A member of the Basiji militia, an Iranian paramilitary group, told a *Jerusalem Post* reporter that prison officials in Iran subject young women to rape prior to their executions. It's all perfectly legal. Islamic law prohibits the execution of virgins, so unmarried women sentenced to die are married off to prison guards, followed by their legalized rape. After that cruel crime is committed against them, they are executed.

"I remember hearing them cry and scream after [the rape] was over," the Basiji militia member said. "I will never forget how this one girl clawed at her own face and neck with her finger nails afterwards. She had deep scratches all over her."[51]

And America is not immune from Islamic oppression of women. Sixteen-year-old Christian convert Rifqa Bary ran away from her home in Ohio in 2009. She fled for fear that her Muslim father would carry out an "honor killing" against her because she had left Islam. "He would kill me or send me back to Sri Lanka," she said after arriving in Florida. A custody fight ensued, and Rifqa's Sri Lankan parents' effort to force her to return home failed after she turned 18 and obtained permanent residency status in the U.S.[52]

Rifqa's claim that she would be killed was not unfounded. Other Muslim girls have been killed in the U.S. for adopting Western ways or acting immodestly in the view of their parents. The father of 20-year-old Noor Almaleki ran her over with a car, leaving Noor with severe injuries from which she died. A police investigator said Noor "was run down in broad daylight by her father who was angry that she had become too Westernized and did not want to accept a marriage her father had arranged for her in the family's native Iraq."[53]

World history and modern culture suggest that we are far, far away from true gender equality. Every major historical incident of one gender being persecuted by another is a case of women being persecuted by men.

SEXUAL ABUSE

The high incidence of rape and sexual violence inside our borders is the most alarming illustration of how men abuse and harm women in the U.S. There were an estimated 83,425 forcible rapes reported to law enforcement in 2011,[54] but that number grossly understates the reality. The CDC's 2010 National Intimate Partner and Sexual Violence Survey (NISVS) found that 1.3 million women said they had been raped in the prior year.[55] According to the results provided by this national telephone survey:

- Nearly 1 in 5 women have been raped in their lifetime.
- 1 in 6 women have been stalked during their lifetime.

- 1 in 4 women have been the victim of severe physical violence by an intimate partner.

The problem of domestic violence is so pervasive that the National Coalition Against Domestic Violence calls it an "epidemic affecting individuals in every community, regardless of age, economic status, race, religion, nationality or educational background."[56] Some 85 percent of all domestic violence victims are women.[57]

Pornography is almost ubiquitous in American culture. It is the most viewed subject online, according to *Time* magazine writer Pamela Paul, who reports that "66% of 18-34-year-old men visit a pornographic site every month."[58] The effects are altogether negative. Porn teaches men to regard women as sex objects and lowers the threshold to violence against women. So-called "adult entertainment" is linked to:

- Seeing women as sex toys: A 2009 study used MRI scans of men who viewed pornography to conclude that porn viewing led men to see women as sexual objects.[59]
- Divorce and Infidelity: Those who have seen an X-rated movie in the last year are "25.6% more likely to be divorced, 65.1% more likely to report having had an extramarital affair, [and] 8.0% less likely to report having a 'very happy' marriage (if they are still married)...."[60]
- Sexual Violence: A survey of college men at a midwestern university found that "men who view pornography are significantly less likely to intervene as a bystander, report an increased behavioral intent to rape, and are more likely to believe rape myths."[61] Executed serial killer Ted Bundy, who murdered at least 28 women, said his sadistic behavior found its origin in his addiction to hard-core pornography. One of Bundy's last victims was a 12-year-old girl, whose body he dumped in a pigsty.[62]

I'm not saying that every man in world history has seen women as less than equal and treated them as such. There are numerous institutions and men throughout history that have worked tirelessly for equal rights for women.

However, we must still draw a sobering conclusion: Throughout history, men in power have had a tendency to persecute women, limit their freedoms and powers, and use them for their own devices. This is accomplished through either political or social actions (customs and laws that limit freedoms) or through passive inaction (sitting by and letting women bear society's burdens or blaming them for society's ills). In America today, the number of women suffering abuse at the hands of men is staggering.

Abortion is a manifestation of man's proclivity to exploit women taken to the extreme. Let's now look at how abortion allows men to carry out their grand social plans, as well as exercise their private passions, without commitment or responsibility.

CHAPTER 4

A WOMAN'S RIGHT – MADE LEGAL BY MEN

While our society trumpets abortion as a woman's right and wants to make sure men have no say in it, it is remarkable just how few women were involved in the rise and acceptance of the practice. Considering today's social view that abortion is a right just for females, men certainly had a lot to do with making sure that right was adopted and passed into law.

In order to understand how men were involved with abortion's 1973 legalization in America, let's first take note that this is not the first time America has faced an abortion crisis.

ABORTION IN THE 19TH CENTURY

While many think abortion has only been rampant in America since the 1970s, abortion was common in the 1800s. Detailed statistics are not available, but Edwin Moses Hale, a physician, claimed in 1867 that "two-thirds of the number of conceptions occurring in the United States, and many other civilized countries, are destroyed criminally."[63] Marvin Olasky, author of *Abortion Rites: A Social History of Abortion in America*, estimates that 160,000 abortions were committed annually during the 1860s, a period when 27 million people lived in America.[64] If the same rate of abortion prevailed today, some 1.86 million abortions would take place each year, given our population of 314 million (instead of the current 1.2 million abortions annually).

In September 1876, another doctor, Augustus Kinsley Gardner, wrote

We look with a shudder upon the poor ignorant Hindoo woman, when from the love for her child which agonizes her mother's heart, in the fervor of her religious enthusiasm sacrifices her beloved offspring at the feet of Juggernaut or in the turbid waves of the sacred Ganges, yet we have not a pang, nor even a word of reprobation, for the human sacrifices of the unborn thousands annually immolated in the city of New York before the blood-worshiped Moloch of fashion.[65]

Though men are primarily responsible for the abortion practice in America today, men were once heavily involved with stemming the abortion tide in the 1800s, as state after state addressed the practice.

Not that abortion had been protected by law. The first abortion-related conviction in America came in 1652 in Maryland, when a Captain William Mitchell was convicted of "adultery, fornication, and murtherous intention" after he forced his 21-year-old bondservant, pregnant with his child, to drink an abortifacient.[66] Such cases were apparently not common. A more common resolution to out-of-wedlock pregnancies was infanticide at birth.

Olasky cites 51 infanticide convictions in Massachusetts between 1670 and 1807. But as abortion became more frequent, state legislators responded with statutes to protect the unborn and punish the perpetrators. By 1868, 30 states had criminalized abortion. Twenty-seven of those state laws, Olasky writes, "punished attempts to induce abortion before quickening."[67]

So while illegal, abortion still became increasingly common in the 1800s. Three groups of people engaged in the social war over abortion, and, over the course of 40 or 50 years, achieved some measure of success protecting women and the unborn that would last for a century.

FEMINISTS

Feminists, journalists, and doctors came together in a loose alliance to help America understand the social, medical, and emotional destruction wrought by abortion.

"Most people are unaware that anti-abortion laws enacted in the latter half of the 19th century were a result of advocacy efforts by feminists, who worked in an uneasy alliance with the male-dominated medical profession and the mainstream media," writes Feminists for Life president Serrin Foster. "These women, who had no rights of their own, were equally concerned about the rights of other oppressed groups, such as slaves, children and the unborn."[68]

Unlike many 21st century feminists, early feminists were strongly opposed to abortion and actively worked for its demise.

Noted feminist Elizabeth Cady Stanton understood that abortion devalued women and increased the gender equality gap:

> Abortion is to be classed, as with the killing of newborns, as infanticide.... There must be a remedy even for such a crying evil as this [abortion]. But where shall it be found, at least where to begin, if not in the complete enfranchisement and elevation of women?[69]

Mary Ann Glendon, the Learned Hand Professor of Law at Harvard University, explains that early feminists fighting for women's rights saw that "the ready availability of abortion would facilitate the sexual exploitation of women." They "regarded free love, abortion and easy divorce as disastrous for women and children."[70]

Perhaps the most well-known early champion of women's rights, Susan B. Anthony, fully understood the negative impact of abortion on women. She argued persuasively that pro-abortion men were greatly at fault for the harm wrought on women.

> I deplore the horrible crime of child-murder. We want prevention, not merely punishment. We must reach the root of the evil. It

[abortion] is practiced by those whose inmost souls revolt from the dreadful deed. All the articles on this subject that I have read have been from men. They denounce women as alone guilty, and never include man in any plans for the remedy.... No matter what the motive, love of ease, or a desire to save from suffering the unborn innocent, the woman is awfully guilty who commits the deed, but, oh! thrice guilty is he who drove her to the desperation which impelled her to the crime.[71]

Years later, feminists still understood that abortion demeaned and degraded women. Celebrated feminist Alice Paul, who drafted the Equal Rights Amendment in 1923, opposed abortion. She called abortion "the ultimate exploitation of women."[72] Evelyn Judge, a lifelong friend of Paul's, said Paul, who died in 1977, once referred to abortion as "killing unborn women."[73]

Contrast that with 1970s feminism, which saw sexual freedom as liberation for both genders. Harvard professor Glendon remarked it "was a puzzling combination of two things that do not ordinarily go together: anger against men and promiscuity; man-hating and man-chasing."[74]

JOURNALISTS

Nineteenth-century members of the press were not silent in expressing their views about abortion. John McDowall, an Amherst- and Princeton-educated Christian worker in New York City, founded the Magdalen Society to shelter seduced and abandoned women. In 1833, he established a monthly magazine, *McDowall's Review*, to detail the reality and magnitude of seduction, prostitution, and abortion in Gotham. He revealed that "thousands of children are murdered. Dead infants are frequently found; sometimes in privies, wells, sewers, ponds, docks...."[75] His aggressive reporting of New York's sensual underside angered many. A grand jury rebuked him for creating a "nuisance" that was "degrading to the character of our city."[76]

After McDowall died in 1836, the *National Police Gazette*, led by editor George Wilkes, pledged to provide "full expositions of the infamous practices of abortionists." In an 1846 editorial Wilkes promised that the *Gazette* would "follow up this business until New York is rid of those child destroyers."[77] The campaign continued over the next two decades, but the *Gazette* had more "readership than prestige," according to historian Marvin Olasky, and did not succeed at igniting public furor against the abortion trade.

In 1870, *New York Times* editor Louis Jennings started an anti-abortion crusade with an editorial, "The Least of These Little Ones," in which he protested that "(the) perpetration of infant murder … is rank and smells to heaven. Why is there no hint of its punishment?" Jennings commissioned an investigation in which a reporter and "lady friend" visited abortionists, posing as a couple in need of their services. The resulting report told readers that "thousands of human beings" are "murdered before they have seen the light of this world."[78]

Yes; that was in *The New York Times*.

Not all newspapers took an aggressive stance against abortion, but the few that did had a measurable impact on American views and attitudes.

DOCTORS

In the medical community, certain courageous men rose up, acknowledged the devastation of abortion, and worked tirelessly to promote change in America.

Horatio Robinson Storer, M.D., was a leader in the doctor's crusade against abortion. Storer, one of America's first gynecologists, urged the American Medical Association to call for more demanding laws against abortion. As chairman of the AMA Committee on Criminal Abortion, he led preparation of a "Report on Criminal Abortion" that was presented to the Association in 1859.

The report reviewed the scope of abortion in the U.S. and called for action. It read,

> Our duty is plain. If, by any act, we can effect aught towards the suppression of this crime, it must be done. In questions of abstract right, the medical profession do not acknowledge such words as

expediency, time service, cowardice. We are the physical guardians of women; we, alone, thus far, of their offspring *in utero*. The case is here of life or death—the life or death of thousands—and it depends, almost wholly, upon ourselves.

As a profession we are unanimous in our condemnation of the crime. Mere resolutions to this effect, and nothing more, are therefore useless, evasive, and cruel.

If to want of knowledge on a medical point, the slaughter of countless children now steadily perpetrated in our midst, is to be attributed, it is our duty, as physicians, and as good and true men, both publicly and privately, and by every means in our power, to enlighten this ignorance. [79]

The AMA unanimously accepted the report, which included recommendations for improving laws against abortion. The report and recommendations were sent to the U.S. President, as well as legislatures of each state and territory. It "described the high and increasing rate of criminal abortion, which led to the deaths of 'hundreds of thousands,' and called for the legislators of the state or territory to pass stringent laws to reduce these deaths."[80]

Storer was also active in saving unborn lives through his own literary output. While pursuing legal protection for the unborn, he also actively worked in the lives of families. He published a series of medical journal articles on abortion in *Why Not? A Book for Women*. The book went through four editions and was used by other physicians to counsel women considering abortion. In 1897, Storer cited the role his book had played in helping women to understand the moral and physical implications of abortion. Hundreds of women had changed their minds, he wrote, and were "induced to permit their pregnancy to accomplish its full period."[81]

Storer expressed sympathy for women and pointed out the horror caused by the failure of the medical community to speak out. "The truth is," he wrote, "that our silence has rendered all of us accessory to the crime, and now that the time has come to strip down the veil, and apply the searching caustic or knife to this foul sore in the body politic, the physician needs courage as well as his patient, and may well overflow with regretful sympathy."[82]

Some of Storer's views and approaches limited his effectiveness. However, he was successful at building momentum in the medical community, and numerous other doctors would join him in his stand against abortion. While other doctors stayed silent or were abortionists themselves, the anti-abortion group of doctors was able to effect change in American culture and state legislatures.

The efforts of early feminists, doctors, and the media brought success for life-affirming proponents. Frederick Dyer, who wrote the book-length chronicle, *The Physicians' Crusade Against Abortion*, recounts, "By 1880, nearly every state and territory had new legislation that made it a serious crime to induce abortions unless the mother's life was in danger. Most of these stringent state laws against abortion were virtually unchanged until *Roe v. Wade* overturned them in 1973."[83]

With laws in place, abortion historian James Mohr wrote, "Between 1880 and 1900 the practice apparently declined in proportion to the total population from what it had been between 1840 and 1880."[84]

APATHY SETS IN

Though men and women joined together to protect America from abortion through social and legislative action, apathy eventually set in. The legislative victories attained by 1880 would stand for almost 100 years, but cracks in the system became evident soon after the laws were passed.

After all, laws were one thing. Prosecution was another. For example, abortionists freely offered their services in the *San Francisco Examiner* during the 1880s and 1890s. The same was true in other cities, including Chicago and St. Louis. Olasky tells about Chicago doctor Rudolph Holmes, who led a 1904 Chicago Medical Society campaign launched to persuade newspapers to "discontinue criminal advertisements or [induce] them to edit the most flagrant violators."[85]

The effort succeeded in ridding Chicago newspapers of abortion solicitations and was imitated in other cities.[86] Still, as Holmes recognized, any victory in the battle was only temporary: "Now that the advertisements are removed the work of the Committee in the future will be to see that they are kept out; in the course of time they undoubtedly will reappear in a new guise...."[87]

Around the turn of the century, the medical profession was wavering in its opposition to abortion. In 1906, the *Journal of the American Medical Association* published Dr. Henry Marcy's assertion that "the product of early impregnation is of so little importance that abortion will not be seriously established as a criminal offense."[88] Dr. William Robinson told a 1911 gathering of the Eastern Medical Society that it was right for unmarried women to abort in certain circumstances. He came out for abortion legalization in the early 1930s, stating that it was "better to permit the removal of a few inanimate cells" than to have "unwanted" children born.[89]

In 1936, Missouri gynecologist Dr. Frederick Taussig wrote *Abortion, Spontaneous and Induced*, a 536-page treatment of the abortion issue praised by *Time* magazine as an "authoritative" and "milestone text."[90] Historian Marvin Olasky called it the "most influential pro-abortion book of the 1930s" and noted that Taussig endorsed legal abortion for instances when "the mother is physically depleted by childbearing and poverty" or "clearly irresponsible."[91] Taussig claimed that 8,000 to 10,000 women died annually from abortion and formulated an argument for abortion that would be used in decades to come, contending "that more consideration must be given to the right of women to control their own bodies."[92]

Taussig's numbers were faulty. Six years later, he confessed that his 1936 book, which also claimed that 681,000 abortions occurred annually, had used "the wildest estimates as to the number of abortions and the number of abortion deaths."[93] He gave a new estimate at a 1942 medical conference of no more than 5,000 abortion deaths annually, but that claim was not tied to any hard statistical evidence either. In any case, the danger to women from abortion dropped sharply after the introduction of penicillin in the mid-1940s. So much so that whatever the true number of abortion-related maternal deaths in 1942, by 1957 Planned Parenthood reported just 260 deaths linked to abortion in America.[94]

The same 1942 National Committee on Maternal Health-sponsored conference where Taussig cut his abortion death estimate by half heard support for abortion, with one speaker suggesting, "the ultimate decision should be hers."[95] At a 1955 Planned Parenthood conference on abortion, Yale psychiatry professor Theodore Lidz declared, "[A]bortion is preferable to the birth of a child that might be injurious to the well-being of the mother...."[96] Participants at the Planned Parenthood gathering concluded that the "mounting approval of psychiatric, humanitarian, and eugenic indications for the legal termination of pregnancy" justified a more relaxed legal environment.[97]

While medical professionals refashioned their attitudes toward abortion, the press shifted its approach, as well. Nineteenth century coverage by the *New York Times* and the *National Police Gazette* had given readers sensational and lurid accounts of predatory abortionists who enriched themselves at the cost of the lives of young women. That changed in the 1930s and 1940s as newspaper accounts distinguished between mercenary and corrupt abortionists and the more humanitarian sort who committed abortion out of compassion. The press, Olasky writes, began to present abortion as an issue in which the "problem was not abortion but the 'unscrupulous abortionist.'"[98]

One of the most evocative and influential events, which generated national press coverage and presented abortion in a sympathetic light, was the case of Mrs. Sherri Finkbine, a pregnant Arizona mother of four. Fearful that the thalidomide in her sleeping pills would create shortened limbs or other defects in her unborn child, Finkbine unsuccessfully sought an abortion in Arizona and ultimately traveled to Sweden for the procedure. The press played up her "plight," and an *Atlanta Constitution* editorial recommended that the "nation ought to have a look at their abortion laws in light of what they did to her."[99] A late 1962 Gallup Poll found that 52 percent of respondents thought Finkbine had "done the right thing" in aborting her child, while 32 percent disagreed with her and 16 percent had no opinion.[100]

Three years later, the *New York Times* came out for liberalized abortion laws, editorializing that limiting abortion to instances aimed at saving the life of the mother "is certainly an example of man's inhumanity to man—or, more directly, to woman."[101]

TURNING BACK TO ABORTION

In the late 1960s, these shifts in attitude led to the relaxation of state abortion laws. Unlike their predecessors, feminists were recruited by men to support abortion.

Abortion laws softened in 1967 as Colorado, California, and North Carolina all passed model legislation legalizing abortion for pregnancies that resulted from rape or incest, for life-threatening situations, and for pregnancies of severely handicapped children. Another nine states would enact similar legislation by 1970: Arkansas, Delaware, Georgia, Kansas, Maryland, New Mexico, Oregon, South Carolina, and Virginia.[102]

The first state to offer unrestricted abortions was New York in 1970. Abortion was now legal there during the first 24 weeks of pregnancy. Hawaii, Alaska, and Washington soon followed. One year later, in 1971, the famed *Roe v. Wade* case first came to trial. When the verdict was handed down in 1973, all state laws regulating abortion were stricken, and abortion on demand became the uniform standard across all 50 states.

RACE TOWARDS LEGALIZATION

How did abortion's legalization come so swiftly? How did we move from the near-universal prohibition on abortion to abortion on demand across the entire nation?

Dr. Bernard Nathanson, a prominent figure in the abortion rights movement, provides tremendous insight into the strategy behind the success.

He met journalist Lawrence Lader, later called the father of the abortion-rights movement by feminist Betty Friedan,[103] at a dinner party in 1967, where they discovered their mutual passion for abortion. "We began to talk, and the conversation lasted eight years," Nathanson recalled. "[I]n that span of time, every abortion law in the United States was struck down, the lines between pro- and anti-abortionists were drawn, and the battle joined."[104]

He and Lader co-founded NARAL (originally the National Association for the Repeal of Abortion Laws and now known as NARAL Pro-Choice America), which became the primary organization in the fight to legalize abortion. Nathanson remembers Lader met him "at the right moment":

> I was upset over the health hazard from illegal abortion, and had moved from disillusionment to cynicism to anger at the inequity and hypocrisy in the abortion business.... Lader never misrepresented his radical purpose: total abolition of abortion restrictions.... It did not seem a time for careful analysis of the issues.[105]

Lawrence Lader's crusade to legalize abortion stemmed from Margaret Sanger, the leading figure in the birth control movement. He wrote an authorized biography of Sanger in 1955 and said the Planned Parenthood founder "undoubtedly was the greatest influence on my life." Sanger's belief in "inviolable personhood" led him to believe that the mother has the sole right over what happens inside her body and that she "controlled the fetus she was nurturing."[106]

Betty Friedan, mother of the modern feminist movement, once asked Lader why he took up the cause of abortion legalization. It was because of Sanger, Lader explained, quoting from Sanger's 1920 work, *Woman and the New Race*: "No woman can call herself free who does not own and control her own body. No woman can call herself free until she can choose consciously whether she will or will not be a mother."[107]

For Lader, the right to abortion was a moral cause on par with the abolition of slavery in the 1800s. "Both involved fundamental moral and religious positions that collided with the entrenched interests of their time," he wrote. And both, he added, "had been created by laws which were blatantly in conflict with basic rights seemingly protected by the Constitution...."[108]

Lader, who gave much of his life to rewriting America's abortion law and expanding access to abortion, argued that laws against abortion "denied women control over their own bodies and procreation by forcing them to bear children against their will."[109] He gave little attention, if any, to the moral status of the unborn and his or her right to be born.

Lader's influential 1966 book, *Abortion*, was a sweeping survey of "the laws and practices governing abortion in the U.S. and around the world." Justice Harry Blackmun cited Lader's book eight times in his 1973 Supreme Court ruling overturning all abortion laws in the U.S. and awarding women the right to choose to end the lives of their unborn children.

The leading figures behind the abortion legalization movement were predominantly male. Abortion historian David Garrow writes that Pat Maginnis, a California woman actively working to repeal abortion laws in the 1960s, "rued the low level of activity on behalf of liberalization, particularly by women, and told [American Civil Liberties Union cofounder] Morris Ernst that 'the men have given us the greatest support.'"[110]

Lader realized he needed women's voices. Nathanson sheds light on how Lader recruited women into the effort to legalize abortion. He recounts how Lader remarked, "If we're going to move abortion out of the books and into the streets, we're going to have to recruit the feminists.'"[111]

Nathanson initially thought that was a mistake: "I figured that if the feminists appeared to take over, the necessary abortion reform would be dismissed by moderates without a fair hearing. I was dead wrong, of course. Lader's marriage with the feminists was a brilliant tactic."[112]

Nathanson and Lader had a specific agenda, the legalization of abortion, but realized they needed to use the appropriate women to gain acceptance in the various states. The question became, then, would the face of the organization be male or female?

"For president, we needed someone pledged to activism and politically astute," Nathanson wrote. "Of course it had to be a woman, though Larry figured to actually run N.A.R.A.L. as chairman of the Executive Committee."[113]

In other words, men would continue to run the organization, while a woman was to be the public face of it. Nathanson recalled their political calculations:

"We've got to keep the women out in front," [Larry] asserted. "You know what I mean."

Yes, I did. And that made eminent political sense, too.

"And some blacks. Black women especially. Why are they so damn slow to see the importance of this whole movement to themselves?"[114]

Even the honorary officers "had to be women, not only to solidify our ties to the feminists, but to rally politically uncommitted women," Nathanson writes. He and Lader "must have sifted through fifty or more names for honorary president" seeking a "white Establishment figure … and also a black … and also a female." [115] Ultimately, Shirley Chisholm, the first black woman elected to Congress, and Dr. Lester Brimlow, president of the American Public Health Association, were tabbed to share the honorary presidency.

Lader and Nathanson recruited Betty Friedan, the co-founder in 1966 of the National Organization of Women, to "join us in the [abortion] revolution,"[116] and she joined the founding board of NARAL.

Recall that 19th century feminists were staunchly against abortion; they realized abortion harmed and exploited women. The 20th century feminist movement did not, at first, support abortion either. Rosemary Oelrich Bottcher, a past president of Feminists for Life, writes:

The first edition of Betty Friedan's seminal book, *The Feminine Mystique*, did not even mention abortion. Legalizing abortion was not on the newborn NOW's list of issues. In his 1979 book, *Aborting America*, Dr. Nathanson recalled Lader saying, "… Friedan has got to put her troops into this thing—while she still has control of them."

When I met Nathanson at the National Right to Life convention in June of 1986, he told me that they convinced the leaders of NOW that easy access to legal abortion was essential to ameliorating the problems that were thwarting the well-being of women, the problems that Friedan had identified in her book.

"We got them to see legal abortion as a civil rights issue, a basic women's rights issue," Nathanson explained.[117]

Thus men conspired to successfully convince leading feminists to include abortion on their agenda as a fix to their other feminist concerns.

Though Friedan would live out the rest of her days as a supporter of abortion, she became critical of NARAL's and NOW's politicized focus on it. "To my mind," she wrote in 2000, "there is far too much focus on abortion.... [I]n recent years I've gotten a little uneasy about the movement's narrow focus on abortion as if it were the single, all-important issue for women, when it's not."[118]

In 1981, Friedan even suggested that feminists "join forces with all who have true reverence for life, including Catholics who oppose abortion, and fight for the choice to have children."[119]

Other writers and historians recognize that the abortion agenda was driven by men who, in turn, convinced and used women to gain support and credibility. "Elitist men have always been the demographic most strongly in support of unrestricted abortion, though they needed vocal women to do their bidding," observes writer Stella Morabito.[120]

In 1971, demographer Judith Blake looked at abortion and public opinion from 1960 to 1970 and reached the surprising conclusion that abortion legalization is not most supported by the "less advantaged and by women." Instead, "Legalized abortion is supported most strongly by the non-Catholic, male, well-educated 'establishment.'"[121] Blake also said, with some understatement, "Upper-class men have much to gain and very little to lose by an easing of legal restrictions against abortion."[122]

And so America, which had fought to protect women and children from abortion in the 1800s, capitulated on that effort in the 1900s. And the effort to legalize abortion was primarily and aggressively driven by men.

The question is, "why?" Dr. Nathanson had his reason, and it was somewhat idealistic—he was concerned about the health and well-being of women getting "back-alley" abortions. He saw the legalization of abortion as a means to protect women's health.

Still, Nathanson, the co-founder of NARAL, later had a change of heart and spent his later years denouncing abortion. He worked to restore America to a culture that respected both women and the unborn.

Were all men as altruistic as Nathanson? Were men fighting so hard for abortion because they were concerned about women's health?

Was it for women's rights? Were these courageous men who saw abortion as a means to elevate women bringing them to true equality with men?

Or was it something else? Were there other agendas behind man's insistence on creating an abortion culture in America?

MEN
OPPRESS
WITH IT

CHAPTER 5

WEEDING
THE GARDEN

While a few men were truly concerned about women's health and saw the legalization of abortion as a means to protect women, the overwhelming majority of male abortion advocates had other motivations: social change and personal sexual behaviors.

On the societal level, the two primary drivers of abortion are population control and eugenics, which often go hand in hand. On the personal level, the driver is male sexual freedom from responsibility or consequence. Women are either being used to advance social agendas or they are being used as sex objects. In either case, women are being exploited as tools to further suggest mostly male agendas.

Population control is the process of maintaining or slowing population growth by decree or practice. China's One Child Policy is an example of population control, in which a portion of Chinese families face fines or worse if they have more than one child. In this case, the Chinese government is enforcing the policy on its own people.

Eugenics is the applied science of weeding out less desirable populations in favor of more desirable populations. In Western history, it generally refers to intentionally decreasing or eliminating a particular race. In recent history, the Nazi holocaust is a well-known, egregious example of applied eugenics.

Eugenics is basically an extension or subset of population control. The rise of abortion in America can be tied directly to both of these social agendas.

"Civil libertarians and feminists were certainly in the picture when it came to the legalization of abortion, but in many cases they were handy instruments of the eugenicists and population controllers," writes Mary Meehan, a senior editor of *Human Life Review*. Abortion advocates had deep-pocketed friends, receiving "enormous aid from the American establishment or 'power elite.'"[123]

Understanding man's role in the legalization of abortion in America requires a closer look at the eugenics movement. For that we turn our attention to the one billion dollar non-profit phenomenon known as Planned Parenthood.

MARGARET SANGER

In 1916, a soft-spoken, passionate female activist opened up the very first birth control center in New York City. Not only did she and a group of friends coin the term "birth control," she went on to start an organization known as the American Birth Control League in 1922. That organization eventually became Planned Parenthood, the most powerful name in birth control and abortion.

Her name was Margaret Sanger, and she was one of the very few prominent female leaders in the movement towards legal abortion, so her background is worth reviewing. In fact, men with both social and personal abortion agendas heavily influenced her views, approach, and tactics.

Sanger started her career as a nurse, working with extremely poor populations. She viewed unplanned children as a core cause of poverty, misery, disease, and death. Poor women pleaded with her to help them limit their families, whether it was for their own physical health, the economic survival of their families, or their own mental well-being. After giving up nursing, she committed her life to educating women about birth control, so they were empowered to dictate the size of their families. She saw birth control as a necessary and vital remedy to numerous social ills.

Sanger, the publisher of *The Birth Control Review* and, before that, *The Woman Rebel*, was also a tireless champion of eugenics. She wanted to rid society of "human weeds" and wrote, in 1925, "We must clear the way for a better world; we must cultivate our garden."[124]

Birth control was her original method of choice, but her views broadened over the years. She endorsed the segregation of "every feeble-minded girl or woman ... especially of the moron class" during their fertile years and concluded in her 1922 book, *The Pivot of Civilization*, that sterilization was an even better option. Since "segregation carried out for one or two generations would give us only partial control of the problem," she wrote, "... we prefer the policy of immediate sterilization, of making sure that parenthood is absolutely prohibited to the feeble-minded."[125]

"The most urgent problem," according to Sanger, "is how to limit and discourage the over-fertility of the mentally and physically defective." And coercion, she made clear, was a tool to be considered: "Possibly drastic and Spartan methods may be forced upon American society if it continues complacently to encourage the chance and chaotic breeding that has resulted from our stupid, cruel sentimentalism."[126]

Sanger was not alone in her extreme eugenic views, nor did she arrive at her conclusions on her own. The founding board of the Birth Control League included at least two male eugenicists, Lothrop Stoddard, and C. C. Little. Stoddard was the author of *The Rising Tide of Color Against White World-Supremacy*, a startling book which divided humanity by color—whites, yellows, blacks, browns, and reds. In it, he warned of a "dreaded" tide of color, which would "swamp whole populations and turn countries now white into colored man's lands irretrievably lost to the white world."[127] Little was a president of the American Eugenics Society.

Another Birth Control League board member was American Eugenics Society co-founder Harry Laughlin. He also served as director of the Eugenics Records Office, America's first major eugenics research institution, from its inception in 1910 to 1939, when it closed its doors.

Over in Britain, eugenicists George Bernard Shaw and H.G. Wells, who wrote the foreword to Sanger's book, *The Pivot of Civilization*, were influential friends of Sanger.

HAVELOCK ELLIS

However, the most profound male influence on Sanger was British sexologist Havelock Ellis. A prolific author on human sexuality, Ellis wrote the six-volume *Studies in the Psychology of Sex* and authored the first British medical textbook on homosexuality. He married at 32 years of age, though it was an unconventional relationship. His wife was a lesbian,[128] and they spent much of their time in separate residences.[129] He was also a eugenicist who served as president of the Galton Institute and vice president of the Eugenics Education Society.

In order to understand Havelock Ellis, it's important to note his connection to Francis Galton, of whom Ellis was a "beloved disciple."[130] Galton's name is familiar to evolutionists, as Galton was the cousin of Charles Darwin, the author of *On the Origin of Species by Means of Natural Selection, or the Preservation of Favoured Races in the Struggle for Life* (later shortened to *On the Origin of Species*). Galton was deeply impacted by Darwin's work, and Darwin's evolutionary theory wove its way into Galton's mindset and writings. The original title of Darwin's work displays the natural tie of evolutionary theory to eugenics, as the latter is based on the preservation of some races and the diminishment of others.

Ellis, heavily influenced by Galton, adopted a very similar philosophy. Darwin's survival of the fittest approach is a necessary key in eugenics, but instead of operating by blind chance, the genetically well-endowed manage the human stock for optimal outcomes. Ellis discussed one way to do so in "The Sterilization of the Unfit," an article that appeared in 1909 in the first issue of the *British Eugenics Review*.[131] In 1912, Ellis advocated comprehensive record-keeping of "all personal facts, biological and mental, normal and morbid ... if we are to have a real guide as to those persons who are most fit, or most unfit to carry on the race."[132]

He advocated the practice of voluntary sterilization of the weak-minded, claiming that "the feeble minded, realising their own weakness, are willing and even anxious to be in this way protected against themselves."[133]

Havelock Ellis and Margaret Sanger would form an intimate friendship that lasted for years, during which he was both her "mentor and lover," according to Sanger biographer Madeline Gray.[134] After Ellis died in 1939, Sanger did a radio interview and extolled his character and contributions. She recalled with reverent awe first meeting him at his home in England in 1914. When Ellis opened the door, "He seemed like a god, with his tall, slender figure, and his great shock of white hair, his massive head, his wide expressive mouth and deep-set eyes...."[135]

Sanger was taken by Ellis' staunch devotion to women's rights and their liberation, saying in the interview that he "helped to usher in a new day of womankind.... He threw the weight of his vast knowledge and influence into advancing the cause of women's freedom, and to women everywhere he seemed a heaven-sent liberator."[136]

By Sanger's own admission, Ellis had a profound impact on her education, studies, and approach to eugenics. The British eugenicist, she said, "guided my early studies and directed my reading for a year and a half in that famous historical spot, the British Museum," where she met regularly with him.[137]

WAS SHE OR WASN'T SHE?

During their time together, Sanger leaned heavily on Ellis to help her craft her strategy related to birth control and eugenics. He persuaded her, as a tactical move, to drop her support for abortion, telling her that industrial society was not ready to cross that threshold.[138]

Before taking Ellis' advice, Sanger had already announced the "right to destroy" and published a pamphlet treating abortion as a form of birth control. Sanger announced in 1914 what she called the "Rebel Woman Claim," which included the "Right to be an unmarried mother," the "Right to create," and the "Right to destroy."[139]

She was more explicit in a 16-page pamphlet first published in 1914 called *Family Limitation*. For women who suspected that conception had occurred, Sanger recommended drinking quinine—a dangerous prescription, which can lead to renal failure—to "prevent the ovum from making its nest in the lining of the womb." But if that fails, "then the only remedy is an abortion."

Sanger went on to endorse abortion as a method of birth control in the same publication, telling readers:

> When once one has been convinced that an abortion is necessary, do not indulge in medicines of any kind. They only weaken the system, and require a much greater length of time to recuperate. Never allow a pregnancy to run over a month. If you are going to have an abortion, make up your mind to it in the first stages, and have it done. On the other hand, there is often a feeling of the strongest desire to continue with the pregnancy. It is for each woman to decide this for herself, but act at once, whichever way you decide.[140]

Advised by Ellis to pursue a more politically expedient course, Sanger later promoted contraception as an allegedly safe alternative to abortion and denounced abortion publicly.[141]

The contradiction between Sanger's initial support of abortion and her autobiography are telling. Originally published in 1938, Sanger noted the dangers and truth about abortion several times and advised against it:

> I still had that naïve trust that when the facts were known, the Government would not willfully condemn millions of women to death, misery, or abortion which left them physically damaged and spiritually crippled.[142]

> All the while their discussions had been proceeding, the people themselves had been and still were blindly, desperately, practicing birth control by the most barbaric methods—infanticide, abortion, and other crude ways.[143]

To each group we explained simply what contraception was; that abortion was the wrong way—no matter how early it was performed it was the taking of a life....[144]

Margaret Sanger was apparently convinced by Havelock Ellis and was not an active abortion promoter or advocate in her later years.

It wasn't women who would aggressively push for the legalization of abortion in America. It was men.

In 1943, the Birth Control Federation of America, a successor organization to Sanger's original American Birth Control League, became the Planned Parenthood Federation of America. But the name change didn't alter its eugenicist agenda. A 1943 Planned Parenthood list of goals stated the group's intent to "foster selective pregnancy...and...seek to offer the eugenically unsound means to avoid bringing offspring into the world who would become social liabilities."[145]

In 1945, another similar outline of Planned Parenthood goals read, in part, "The weak and defective compose an alarming proportion of our present population...." The solution was "providing reliable contraceptive advice for those who, because of disease, defectiveness or deficiency, are unfitted to bear children."[146]

But as Nazi horrors became known in America, public opinion swung against eugenics, requiring its advocates to play their cards much closer to their vests. C. P. Blacker, chosen by Sanger to be the founding president of the International Planned Parenthood Federation, endorsed what he called "crypto-eugenics." He understood that eugenics would only be advanced if the actual agenda was hidden, saying, "You seek to fulfill the aims of eugenics without disclosing what you are really aiming at and without mentioning the word."[147]

Havelock Ellis was very much the master planner behind Sanger's passions, as she herself proudly admitted. And though the "right to destroy," which she endorsed in 1914, was not realized in her lifetime, her successor at Planned Parenthood saw that right arrive with the Supreme Court's 1973 *Roe v. Wade* ruling.

ALAN GUTTMACHER

Just three years after Sanger's death in 1966, Planned Parenthood adopted abortion legalization as a corporate policy. Its president, Dr. Alan Guttmacher, an obstetrician-gynecologist, was, as early as the 1940s, one of the nation's first physicians to move towards legalized abortion. Guttmacher called for liberalizing abortion laws at the American Birth Control Federation's 1942 annual meeting saying, "[T]he patent hypocrisy and holier-than-thou attitude of the medical profession in regard to this problem is revolting."[148]

In 1962, Guttmacher left his post as chief of obstetrics and gynecology at Mt. Sinai Hospital to become Planned Parenthood president. Guttmacher was out in front of his organization on abortion, writing in 1974 that he "took this [abortion legalization] position long before it became Planned Parenthood policy in 1969."[149]

As with almost every man associated with the promotion and legalization of abortion, Guttmacher was a population control and eugenics advocate, serving as a vice president of the American Eugenic Society. Like many others, he was willing to use force to achieve population control. "Each country," he said in 1969, "will have to decide its own form of coercion, and determine when and how it should be employed. At present, the means are compulsory sterilization and compulsory abortion. Perhaps someday a way of enforcing compulsory birth control will be feasible."[150]

Guttmacher observed that it's best to use camouflage when seeking to achieve population control on the international stage: "If you're going to curb population, it's extremely important not to have it done by the damned Yankees, but by the UN. Because the thing is, then it's not considered genocide." As Guttmacher told an interviewer, "If the United States goes to the black man or the yellow man and says slow down your reproductive rate, we're immediately suspected of having ulterior motives to keep the white man dominant in the world. If you send in a colorful UN force, you've got much better leverage."[151]

As Ellis, Sanger, and eventually Guttmacher continued their rise to prominence in the 20th century, other men of tremendous wealth and power were advancing their abortion agendas.

THE MONEY MEN

Billionaire John D. Rockefeller III and military leader/philanthropist Frederick Osborn launched the Population Council in 1952, a foundation that worked diligently to convince government leaders in poor nations that they had population problems. They then provided potential solutions to those governments.

The solutions included distributing intrauterine devices (IUDs) and other contraceptive/abortifacient (abortion causing) devices in third world nations. Though population control was their public concern, their private agenda was eugenics.

Osborn tipped off a correspondent that the Population Council was pursuing a crypto-eugenics agenda by spending large sums on IUDs, adding, "We have felt this could be done far more effectively in the name of Population Control than in the name of eugenics.... Personally, I think it is the most important practical eugenic measure ever taken."[152]

John D. Rockefeller III was a self-proclaimed eugenicist, and it ran in the family. Both his father, John D. Rockefeller Jr., and his grandfather, oil magnate John D. Rockefeller, were members of the American Eugenics Society. John D. Rockefeller III contributed heavily during the Depression years to keep it solvent.

Abortion was also on the Rockefeller agenda. In 1967, John D. Rockefeller III told his sister, "[T]he matter of abortion is the principal remaining area in the population field which has not been given the attention that it should."[153]

In 1970, it was New York Governor Nelson Rockefeller, John D. Rockefeller III's brother, who signed into law a measure allowing abortion for any reason up to six months gestation. Two years later, Governor Rockefeller vetoed a measure to repeal that law.

John D. Rockefeller III also supported the Association for the Study of Abortion, which pressed for the legalization of abortion and included other major eugenicists such as Guttmacher, Harvard Divinity School professor and situation ethics advocate Joseph Fletcher, and abortion statistician Christopher Tietze.

Frederick Osborn was the key strategist of the American Eugenics Society and the first president of the Population Council. Well before surgical abortions became a major issue, Osborn advocated research on chemical abortions and the Population Council's distribution of abortifacient IUDs. His agenda and motivations are clear, as he said in 1974, "Birth control and abortion are turning out to be the great eugenic advances of our time. If they had been advanced for eugenic reasons it would have retarded or stopped their acceptance."[154]

The population control/eugenics movement tied logically and inevitably into abortion. For example, Stanford biology professor and population alarmist Paul Ehrlich issued a warning of coming doom in his 1968 bestseller, *The Population Bomb*. Ehrlich predicted that "hundreds of millions of people are going to starve to death" in the 1970s because of famines tied to overpopulation and listed abortion as one way to defuse the bomb. He argued for the legalization of abortion in the U.S. and wrote that "in many cases abortion is much more desirable than childbirth."[155]

President Richard Nixon appointed a population commission in 1970, which studied the issue for two years and recommended, among other things, public funding for abortion "on request." The chairman of the committee was none other than John D. Rockefeller III, with numerous other Population Council members and eugenicists on the commission or related staff.

The commission, as writer Mary Meehan notes, asked

for more research on fertility control and more subsidy of contraception and sterilization; [it] support[ed] sex education and 'population education' in the schools; and recommend[ed] a national average of two children per couple.[156]

EUGENICS APPLIED TO MINORITIES

Historically, eugenics targeted poor populations and minorities. Though the modern media downplays the role of racism and gender discrimination in eugenics, the words of the movement's founders are quite clear. Francis Galton, for example, wrote in 1904 that "while most barbarous races disappear, some, like the negro, do not"[157] and Sanger associate Lothrop Stoddard issued a dire warning in 1922 about the "rising tide of color against white-world supremacy." Eugenicist Madison Grant's popular book, *The Passing of the Great Race*, inveighed against the "social and racial crime" of interracial marriage and said, "[T]he law against miscegenation [interracial marriage] must be greatly extended if the higher races are to be maintained."[158]

In his landmark 1944 examination of American race relations, Swedish eugenicist Gunnar Myrdal claimed, without a shred of evidence, that "all white Americans agree that, if the Negro is to be eliminated, he must be eliminated slowly so as not to hurt any individual living Negroes."[159]

But how could that slow fade of African Americans from the population be achieved? After dismissing outright elimination, deportation, voluntary emigration, and keeping the black death rate high, Myrdal concludes, "The only possible way of decreasing Negro population is by means of controlling fertility."[160] One option offered by Myrdal in *An American Dilemma* is to provide the African-American population with birth control—lots of it. Myrdal suggests "birth control facilities could be extended relatively more to Negroes than whites."[161]

Margaret Sanger's "Negro Project" was an effort to expand the distribution of contraceptives to African Americans. Her real agenda may have been similar to Myrdal's claim about the common ambition of all whites. In private correspondence with fellow eugenicist Dr. Clarence Gamble, Sanger wrote, "We do not want the word to go out that we want to exterminate the Negro population and the minister is the man who can straighten that idea out if it ever occurs to any of their more rebellious members."[162]

For his part, Gamble proposed recruiting black doctors to serve with ministers as advocates for the birth control campaign. "There is great danger that [the project] will fail because the Negroes think it a plan for extermination," Gamble wrote Sanger. "Hence let's appear to let the colored run it...."[163]

Whatever the motive behind Sanger's birth control initiative to black Americans, it's disturbing to realize that African Americans, who now make up 12.8 percent of the population, have 35.4 percent of all abortions. Even more striking is the fact that the abortion rate—the number of abortions per 1,000 women—is almost four times greater among black women (32.5) than white women (8.5).[164]

One reason for the dramatic difference in abortion rates may be the higher concentration of Planned Parenthood abortion facilities near black neighborhoods, possibly following Myrdal's suggestion. An analysis done by Life Issues Institute researcher Susan Enouen compared the location of Planned Parenthood abortion facilities with Census Bureau data and found that "62% of Planned Parenthood abortion facilities are within walking distance (2 miles) of relatively high African American populations."[165]

Another similar analysis conducted by Life Dynamics checked the zip codes of minority neighborhoods against the locations of abortion facilities and found that 83 percent of facilities that perform or refer for abortions are in minority neighborhoods. As Life Dynamics president Mark Crutcher put it, "The numbers make it clear that the African-American and Hispanic communities have been targeted, and logic makes it clear that this did not happen coincidentally or unintentionally."[166]

POPULATION CONTROL AND WOMEN

Despite the fact that global population growth is slowing and may begin to decline within our lifetime,[167] funding for population control measures seems to be a well that never runs dry. Notable names such as Rockefeller, Ford, Mellon, and Packard are among the many foundations that have historically supported this movement. New money for population control is coming from, among others, Warren Buffet, Bill Gates, Ted Turner, and George Soros.[168] These men and others, including Michael Bloomberg, David Rockefeller, and Oprah Winfrey, gathered in May 2009 for a "billionaires' club" summit to discuss their favorite causes and settled on world population as their primary concern.

One individual at the meeting told the *Times of London*, "This is something so nightmarish that everyone in this group agreed it needs big-brain answers. They need to be independent of government agencies, which are unable to head off the disaster we all see looming."[169]

Aside from the fact that population growth is a non-problem, given that the worldwide fertility rate has plummeted from 6.5 children per family 40 years ago to about 2.5 now,[170] the solutions funded by wealthy population controllers often victimize women. They, along with the poor and non-white people groups, are the typical target of population control measures. As women are the child bearers, any biological or social changes to enforce population or eugenic ideas are almost exclusively aimed at them.

The Population Research Institute, a group that seeks to expose the myth of overpopulation, has quantified the impact on women. A PRI-produced list of 70 population control abuses in 30 countries shows that women have been the targets in 62 of the 70 incidents listed. The abuses listed include sterilization, forced abortion, sex-selection abortion, infanticide, or Depo-Provera injections without informed consent.[171]

STERILIZATION

The recent worldwide history of sterilization shows women are most often the victims. While men have been targeted for sterilization, as in India, where several million men were neutered in the 1970s,[172] women are victimized far more often. The targeting of women and girls to enforce population control is as sad as it is graphic. Sterilization camps in India have been used since the 1970s to reduce India's population growth. A 1994 *Washington Post* report described a camp in Sarsawa, India, where women were given a local anesthesia and then placed on "makeshift operating tables where a doctor dedicates a total of 45 seconds to each patient— slitting open the belly, inserting a laparoscope, tying the fallopian tubes, dipping the laparoscope into a pail of lukewarm water and then moving on to the next patient."

Afterwards, the women were placed in a "dim ward where dozens of women lie side by side on the concrete floor, filling the room with the low moans and quavering wails of excruciating pain." According to the *Washington Post* report, the women "are poor and illiterate, and most are lured to government clinics and camps with promises of houses, land or loans by government officials under intense pressure to meet sterilization quotas."[173]

And this is still going on in India. More than 100 women were sterilized in one day on February 6, 2013, at a government hospital in West Bengal, India. The post-operative recovery took place in an open field near the 60-bed hospital, where the women were stretched out on the ground, exposed to the elements and in plain view of hundreds of onlookers.[174]

In Peru, where then-president Alberto Fujimori imposed population control measures in the late 1990s, Victoria Esperanza Vigo Espinoza was sterilized without her knowledge. She had a C-section, signed a release, and wound up unable to conceive again. "I felt mutilated. That's the truth. My rights as a mother and woman were violated," Vigo said. Hers is not the only case of a Peruvian woman being sterilized without her knowledge. Human rights groups claim there are more than 2,000 documented instances of women whose tubes were tied without their knowledge or consent.[175]

Forced sterilization has also taken place right here in the U.S. The first law allowing for eugenic sterilizations was passed in 1907 in Indiana, and more than 60,000 people were sterilized in 33 states during the 20th century.[176] The documentary *Maafa 21* features an interview with Elaine Riddick, a black woman who was sterilized in 1968 at age 14, after she gave birth to a son conceived by rape. She later learned about the operation, which had been approved by the Eugenics Board of North Carolina. She asked "why they did this to me, and they said I was feeble-minded. I would not be able to take care of myself. I would not be able to tie my shoes, that I was just incompetent."

Riddick, a college graduate, said her son is the owner of his own semi-conductor, real estate, and construction firms. She said the state told her "feeble-mindedness was hereditary, so they sterilized me so I would not produce my kind. Mind you, I am not illiterate nor am I feeble-minded.... To me, they took away all my rights."[177]

In Indonesia, there are documented cases of women who had IUDs inserted at gunpoint.[178] In Africa, a University of Nairobi teaching physician relayed "in gory detail how doctors in Kenya routinely cut women's fallopian tubes during cesarean section operations—without even seeking permission to do so in advance."[179]

China practices coercive IUD insertion, sterilization, and abortion. Fines and government pressure can be levied against families with more than one child. At one house, a husband did not cooperate when authorities told him to have his wife dress and go to the abortion center. So four women on the government team entered the house, struggled with his wife, and then carried her out "in a folded quilt." Two other team members held the husband back when he tried to rescue his wife and unborn child.[180]

Population control and eugenics are obviously not limited to the United States, where forced sterilizations took place long before they were introduced in Nazi Germany or elsewhere. Based on the work of population control and eugenics groups, these measures occur around the world.

There are two key points from this section:

1. The victims of population control and eugenics measures are primarily women. While men (such as the Chinese father mentioned above) suffer emotionally, virtually all physical procedures (sterilization, abortions, and other birth control procedures) are performed on women.
2. The overwhelming majority of people behind the population control and eugenics movements historically have been men. This is not to say that women were uninvolved. But almost all of the key players were men in positions of power and wealth.

Population control and eugenics are tools in the hands of powerful men to achieve worldwide control over various populations they deem unworthy to grow. Most of the time, these are minority, handicapped, or impoverished populations.

If you are a person concerned with the care of the poor, you may well be wondering if population control is a valid tool. After all, Margaret Sanger began her journey promoting birth control because of the intense suffering she saw firsthand in impoverished populations. In her mind, educating women on how to limit the number of children was directly connected to their health and welfare.

There is a key point of distinction here, however. Helping the poor to manage the size of their families through proper education is one thing. Knowledge is power, and education is essential for any poor community to rise out of its condition.

However, is it a solution for a powerful population group to impose non-lethal and lethal birth control on other people? Is it right and fair for one group to force another to limit its population?

Here's why the questions are essential. The logical conclusion to discriminatory birth control is always abortion. As eugenicists in the 1900s discovered, education wasn't enough. Sterilization was the next step and, if that didn't work, the only final solution was abortion.

In the case of America, it was powerful, rich, white men who were behind the legalization of abortion, not women.

But men have another reason to push abortion, and it has nothing to do with worldwide population control or racism.

CHAPTER 6

"I'll Still Love You in the Morning"

A s this review of world history has revealed, men have a habit of using women for their sexual pleasure. Whether through the practices of binding feet, harems, or prostitution; the legal ease of getting a divorce (so a new wife can be acquired); or pornography, men in numerous cultures throughout world history have used their power, money, and influence to satisfy their sexual urges outside of a relationship or environment that is equally beneficial for women.

Obviously, pregnancy is a natural and normal outcome of sexual relations, whether those relations are for one gender's benefit or both.

Throughout the course of American history, unintended pregnancies have been dealt with in a number of ways. Quick "shotgun" weddings were an option, where the father and mother married in haste in order to avoid the once-public shame of an unintended pregnancy.

Sending the woman away for several months was another option. The woman would disappear for a time (perhaps with an excuse of visiting a relative or going to boarding school), give birth to the child, and then return home. The public embarrassment was still prevalent, but the woman didn't have to bear public scorn while pregnant.

Prior to 1973, illegal abortion was also an option.

THE OTHER AMERICAN REVOLUTION

As the sexual revolution of the 1960s exploded and traditional marriage began to erode, men broke the boundaries of sexual control. Abstinence before marriage started to become a public joke, and the concepts of living together and no-fault divorce began to gain public acceptance.

While the sexual revolution is normally associated with the 60s, its actual launch can be dated to 1948, when Indiana University researcher Alfred Kinsey released *Sexual Behavior in the Human Male*, with funding assistance from The Rockefeller Foundation. The bestselling report purported to show that nearly all American men were sexual adventurers who routinely flouted the bounds of marriage. Widely publicized as the verdict of sober science, Kinsey's research claimed that 85 percent of men had sex before marriage and 70 percent used prostitutes. Between 30 and 45 percent of married men had affairs and 10 to 37 percent of men engaged in homosexual encounters.[181]

Kinsey is credited as the "Father of the Sexual Revolution" for his work, but his research was junk science. Aside from being a sexual psychopath who sought gratification in weird ways, including self-circumcision with a pocket knife,[182] Kinsey's findings were unreliable. Dr. Judith Reisman has revealed that Kinsey researchers "based their claims about normal males on a roughly 86 percent aberrant male population including 200 sexual psychopaths, 1,400 sex offenders and hundreds each of prisoners, male prostitutes, and promiscuous homosexuals."[183]

Kinsey also inspired Playboy publisher Hugh Hefner, that famous advocate of unlimited sexual gratification. Hefner, who founded Playboy in 1953, considered himself Kinsey's "pamphleteer, spreading the news of sexual liberation through a monthly magazine."[184] Hefner also worked to legalize abortion through his Playboy Foundation, established in 1965. "We fought for birth control rights and the change in birth control laws, the change in abortion laws, we fought cases to give women the right to choose," Hefner has said.[185]

His magazine came out for abortion's legalization in 1965 and, in 1967, encouraged readers to call legislators in those states then considering a relaxation of legal limits on abortion. The magazine covered abortion law developments and publicized abortion services, providing phone numbers, costs, and other information.[186]

Women, Hefner claims, have been the "major beneficiaries of the sexual revolution." What it achieved, he said, "was give freedom to both sexes not only in the bedroom, but everywhere else."[187]

No-fault divorce was another alleged benefit to both men and women that arrived about the same time as the sexual revolution. California Governor Ronald Reagan signed the nation's first no-fault divorce bill into law in 1969, and the rest of the states followed over the next 15 years. No-fault divorce laws allow one spouse to leave the marriage without evidence of adultery or abandonment by simply claiming discontent based on vague complaints like "mental cruelty" or "incompatibility."

The result has been disastrous. The divorce rate per 1,000 married women in the U.S. more than doubled between 1960 and 1980, jumping from 9.2 to 22.6,[188] as no-fault divorce laws took effect across the nation. Political scientist Stephen Baskerville says easy divorce is the "most direct threat to the family" and says it must be resolved "if civilization is to endure."[189]

Fortified by the "findings" of Kinsey, inflamed with the Playboy philosophy, and given an easy "out" by abortion and no-fault divorce, men have, for the last generation, pursued sexual gratification with reckless abandon. And I do mean reckless:

- The number of couples living together outside marriage jumped seventeenfold from 1960 to 2010.[190]
- Nearly 22 percent of men ages 15-44 have had 15 or more sex partners.[191]
- The illegitimacy rate is now almost 41 percent.[192]
- There are an estimated 20 million new STIs (sexually transmitted infections) annually.[193]

To be sure, women have participated in the process. But, as with the social agendas related to abortion, men have orchestrated the movement and led the charge.

The "problem" with sexual freedom outside marriage is pregnancy. Inside marriage, pregnancy is generally accepted and desired. Outside of marriage, pregnancy is often an unintended consequence of sexual freedom and thus poses a threat to that freedom.

So what do men do when their sexual freedom causes a pregnancy? That pregnancy, which under all normal circumstances results in the birth of a child, brings a whole new set of responsibilities and commitments. As any parent knows, a child brings an enormous amount of change to any family, along with numerous obligations, which weren't present prior to the pregnancy.

JUST A THEORY, MIND YOU

Allow me to propose a theory. What if pregnancy could be terminated so that sexual freedom could be maintained? And what if men had no responsibility for the pregnancy or its termination? And, in the best of all scenarios, what if women actually celebrated the responsibility for pregnancy and its termination and gave men no credit, no right, and no voice in that process?

Abortion is the ultimate "get out of jail free" card for sexually aggressive men. Men can continue having sexual relations with multiple women, refuse to commit to any one woman in marriage, and divorce a woman through no-fault divorce if they aren't sexually or emotionally satisfied. And if, along the way, a woman gets pregnant, the man has avoided all responsibility to that woman for his child. Maybe they cough up a few hundred bucks for the abortion; maybe not.

Is this just a theory? Men wouldn't be so crass, so manipulative, so selfish that they would intentionally use abortion as a way of pursuing their sexual appetites. They wouldn't so easily cast their female partners aside, leaving them to deal with the impact of pregnancy or the typical devastation of abortion. They certainly wouldn't abandon their female partners just because their sex life led to a pregnancy.

Is this the path to elevating the role of women in society?

Ironically, numerous scholars and sociologists readily admit abortion is all about sex. And they candidly confess abortion is really about men having the freedom to do what they want with no consequence.

Catharine MacKinnon, an influential feminist legal scholar, writes that abortion "does not liberate women; it frees male sexual aggression. The availability of abortion removes the one remaining legitimized reason that women have had for refusing sex besides the headache."[194]

And that is why, she notes, "the Playboy Foundation has supported abortion rights from day one" at a level on par with its other *cause célèbre*, "opposition to censorship." As another feminist writer, Andrea Dworkin, put it much more crassly, "Getting laid was at stake."[195] Or as an abortion advocate said at a UN conference, "Let's stop fooling around here. What we're talking about is our right to f*** whoever we want, however we want, whenever we want."[196]

Feminist Dorchen Leidholdt sees it pretty much the same but puts it more politely:

> Sexually liberal men support abortion for women not because they want women to be able to control their bodies but because they know that unrestricted abortions heighten women's availability to men for sex.[197]

The most astonishing thing about all this is that, despite feminist rhetoric about rights and empowerment, abortion deeply wounds women and gives men license to exploit them. Some feminists do understand this.

In recent years, a few have recognized the sheer injustice of asking a woman to abort her child in order to participate fully in society. In the words of the New Zealand feminist author Daphne de Jong: "If women must submit to abortion to preserve their lifestyle or career, their economic or social status, they are pandering to a system devised and run by men for male convenience."[198]

More evidence for this sexual agenda comes from an unwitting source, the Center for Reproductive Rights, which produced a video meant to celebrate *Roe's* fortieth anniversary. Instead, the quickly-pulled piece was a painful self-parody displaying the truth behind abortion rights. The CRR production featured a black actor dressed in a suit before a fireplace, with a glass of liquor and a rose on the table in front of him. He chuckles, leers, and says, as if speaking to *Roe*, "Happy anniversary, baby. Looking good for 40," his voice trailing off in a series of grunts that close with a contented sigh.

This crude video reveals, once more, that male sexual appetite is a primary driver of the abortion rights movement in America.

These examples and quotes are not from life-affirming or family organizations. With the exception of Daphne de Jong, they are from abortion advocates, feminists, and one of the most vocal organizations promoting abortion in America. Beneath the marketing campaigns that promote "choice," "reproductive rights," and "empowering women," lies the real social reason for abortion: men having the freedom to sleep with whoever they want with no legal or social consequence to themselves.

This has been the underlying social reason for abortion for centuries.

Writing in 1871, Dr. John Cowan listed the "licentiousness of the man and the bondage of the woman" as the cause of the "monstrous crime … the murder of the unborn."[199]

Another 19th century doctor summed up the role of sexually liberal men well. Acknowledging that abortion oppresses women, Dr. John Trader argued that the impetus and responsibility for abortion rests with men: "We do not affirm, neither would we have you think for a moment, that the onus of this guilt lies at the feet of women. Far from it. In the majority of cases, they are more sinned against than sinning."[200]

And, as noted earlier, feminist Susan B. Anthony wrote:

I deplore the horrible crime of child-murder.... No matter what the motive, love of ease, or a desire to save from suffering the unborn innocent, the woman is awfully guilty who commits the deed, but, oh! thrice guilty is he who drove her to the desperation which impelled her to the crime.[201]

CHAPTER 7

EDUCATED CHOICE?

At this point, you may be thinking, "So what? So what if men have primarily controlled the promotion and legalization of abortion. Even if men are the 'wizards behind the curtain,' they have still advanced female rights. Women still have the right to choose and, for that, we are grateful to men."

But do women really have that right? Do they have complete freedom to choose abortion or not? Do women get all the facts, medically and emotionally speaking, to make an informed decision? Are they able to independently make that choice, free from the influence and coercion of men?

Sadly, the answer is clearly no. Though it is a woman's right to choose whether or not to abort, the data once again show that men continue to have tremendous influence over that decision. Male coercion, whether active or passive, plays a huge role in the abortion decision.

INFORMED

If women are to be fully empowered, they must be educated. Women have fought for this right in various cultures for good reason. Making decisions from ignorance can have dire consequences.

In America, we strive for female education and equality. Women generally have the same opportunities as men for public or private schooling, collegiate and post-graduate education.

In matters of health, America strongly encourages women to be fully educated about their bodies, how to fight illnesses, how to take care of themselves, and how to protect and defend themselves.

We encourage patients, male and female, to seek second opinions when diagnosed with an illness or injury that requires extensive care. In regard to female health, the medical community seeks to provide mammograms, PAP smears, and numerous other female examinations in order to inform about and protect women from potentially harmful health issues.

Do we provide the same sort of commitment, education, and redundancy when a woman is faced with the decision of whether or not to willfully take the life of another human being? Do we fully disclose to women that the decision to abort very often comes with extremely difficult emotional and physical side effects?

It's one thing to educate women about breast cancer screenings. We all consider this to be vital and necessary. Do we not think that a full education is required if the decision has a life-and-death impact on another human being?

Apparently not.

The Elliot Institute cites research showing that information and counseling are in short supply for women contemplating an abortion. According to these findings, among women considering abortion:[202]

- 54 percent were unsure of their decision, yet 67 percent received no counseling beforehand;[203]
- 84 percent were inadequately counseled beforehand;
- 79 percent were deceived or not told about available resources; and
- many were misinformed by experts about fetal development, abortion alternatives, or risks.

The Elliot Institute also reports that many post-abortive women say they were denied essential personal, family, societal, or economic support.[204] One study, for example, found:

- 64 percent of women who had an abortion said their partner did not provide support;
- Only 20 percent of post-abortive women said their parents were involved in the abortion decision. [205]

Theresa Burke, the founder of Rachel's Vineyard, a ministry that helps men and women find healing after abortion, says the lack of support continues after abortion. While nearly 78 percent of post-abortive women report feeling guilty,[206] the therapeutic safety net is non-existent. There is little in the way of acknowledgement, let alone support.

"The psychological and spiritual agony of abortion is silenced by society, ignored by the media, rebuffed by mental health professionals, and scorned by the women's movement," says Burke. "Post-abortion trauma is a serious and devastating illness which has no celebrity spokeswoman, no made-for-television movie, and no platform for the talk show confessional."[207]

And are women fully educated on the severe risks associated with abortion?

- Women who have abortions are nearly four times more likely to die later from accident-related injuries.[208] One study found that women who had abortions had a 62 percent higher risk of death from all causes than did women who gave birth. Factors leading to death included suicide and accidents.[209]
- Suicide rates six times higher after abortion.[210]
- 65 percent of women suffer trauma symptoms after abortion.[211]

INDEPENDENT?

If we are concerned about women's equality and rights, we should not only be concerned about women being properly informed about abortion, we should also be concerned about their ability to make an abortion decision independent of male coercion.

While the majority of women are not properly informed of their options and, therefore, are often making a life-and-death decision (one that impacts their personal and mental health greatly) without all of the facts, surely women are able to make the decision without male interference? After all, that is true gender equality, is it not?

Once again, women are exploited by men.

- 64 percent of women reported feeling pressured to abort.[212]
- Most felt rushed or uncertain, yet 67 percent weren't counseled.[213]
- Clinics fail to screen for coercion.[214]
- Many times the pressure to abort comes from a male figure, generally the father of the baby or the woman's father. And the pressure is not just emotional.
- Pressure to abort can escalate to violence.[215]
- Homicide is the leading killer of pregnant women.[216]

There are numerous examples of this coercion:[217]

He destroyed our apartment ... and told me to get rid of it. Now! The whole time he cornered me ... throwing things and killing me with his words. The abortion ripped me apart. Any strength I had to leave the abuse was torn away from me.

—Mary

I was a victim of incest at 15.... In spite of the pain and guilt I felt, it was far better to have a baby than the alternative— to kill it. I refused to have an abortion.... My father flew into an uncontrollable rage and demanded that I consent to the abortion.... [The doctor] asked three nurses to hold me while he strapped me to the bed.... I continued to scream that I didn't want an abortion. He told me, "Shut up and quit that yelling!"... I was violated by my father ... I was violated again by the abortionist.

—Denise (not real name)

No one would support me.... The worst day of my life got closer and closer.... I think in more cases than not, it isn't the woman's choice. It should be called "Your Parents' and the Guy's Choice."... I needed someone to tell me that it was possible to keep my baby, but no one did...."

—Amanda

Sometimes the coercion is active and violent. Many times, it is the father's passive approach or simple unwillingness to parent that overpowers a woman's natural desire to nurture and protect her child.

The Guttmacher Institute, a pro-abortion research organization that was originally a branch of Planned Parenthood, conducted a study of 21 post-abortive women who experienced difficulty, including a sense of regret, after the abortion. The study reported that "negative outcomes" followed when the father took a pass on his responsibility for the pregnancy and left the mother "feeling as though she had no other choice."[218]

Another study indicates that the most important factor in a woman's decision to abort a second pregnancy is, rather than poverty, whether the father has been active or passive in the care of a first child. The likelihood of abortion rose significantly, the study found, when women felt that the father was unlikely to "watch the child for a week," "take good care of the child," "watch the child when the mother needs to do things," or if he "does not support the mother's way of raising the child" and "does not respect the schedule and rules" the child is to follow.[219] And, no surprise, the study, published in the *International Journal of Mental Health and Addiction*, also found that marriage made abortion much less likely.[220]

Agreeable fathers who say, "Sure, babe, I'll support your abortion decision, if that's what you want," may see the relationship turn cold and angry afterwards, says researcher Dr. Vincent Rue. "One of the sad realities of abortion," he writes, "is how caring men, who try not to hurt the women they love, in fact hurt them by saying nothing when abortion is first mentioned in the crisis decision-making process."

Men who are passive and compliant toward their abortion-minded mate may wind up facing "a fierce, often denied, undercurrent of resentment stemming from their partner's feelings of abandonment," according to Dr. Rue, who is co-director of the Institute for Pregnancy Loss in Jacksonville, Florida. "Wanting to please, these men are rejected because they were judged deficient in true love for their partners."[221]

That "undercurrent of resentment" surfaced at the Red River Women's Clinic, a Fargo, North Dakota, abortion facility. It's a place, according to a *Time* magazine report, where female patients, who are encouraged to express their feelings in journals, "write about non-supportive husbands and boyfriends and ask God for forgiveness."[222]

Is abortion empowering for women? If they are not fully informed about the risks and potential side effects of abortion, and if they are heavily influenced by males in the abortion decision, just how empowering is it?

INTELLIGENT?

Ironically, it seems like some in our culture think women are too stupid to make an informed decision. They don't want women getting a second opinion from a source that doesn't support abortion.

One woman, commenting on the Online for Life iPhone app mentioned previously, wrote:

> Nothing but judgmental and manipulative means to brainwash woman (sic) by standing behind the cliché catch phrase of "providing options." Using sonogram propaganda to guilt women into "saving a life" further confirms the stupidity of ignorant Bible thumping leaders who continue to take your money so they can create absurd Apps such as these. Keep those prayers coming folks. I'm sure your (sic) saving those babies (sic) lives.

As I was writing this chapter, a news story aired about the 24-hour mandatory waiting period for abortion in my home state of Texas. A pro-abortion state politician complained about the waiting period, claiming it was harmful to women, caused confusion, and put more pressure on women when they have already made up their minds. She said the law runs the risk of manipulating women's minds.

This sentiment is common. Women should not get separate counsel and not have to wait a day or two to consider other options. They are supposedly susceptible to brainwashing and can't make an informed decision. They are too easily manipulated to handle opinions contrary to the abortion provider's.

If a woman is about to have a surgical procedure, do we not want her to have information about all alternatives? Should she not be informed about the possible outcomes of all options? I would think so. We want her to know about the pre-op, post-op, and recovery expectations. We want her to know if there are any holistic or alternative medicines that could assist her. Perhaps her surgery could be avoided with proper diet, exercise, or vitamins. We would all feel a strong commitment to make sure the woman has the opportunity to see her potential surgery and its alternatives from all angles, so she can make the best decision for herself.

And, in the case of abortion, the surgery ends the life of another human being. Not only are we considering the life and well-being of the mother, abortion is a life-and-death decision.

Are women so susceptible to manipulation and brainwashing that they can't sort through the information to make an informed decision?

Apparently women aren't very intelligent, discerning, or wise.

So, are the majority of women properly educated when considering abortion? The data points to a severe lack of appropriate information and counsel.

Are the majority of women making independent decisions regarding abortion? No. In the majority of cases, they are heavily influenced or coerced by others—namely, men.

Are women capable of handling a variety of viewpoints about their abortion decision? Apparently not, as many think they are too dumb or weak to think through contrary viewpoints about abortion, a surgery that verifiably ends the life of another human being.

CHAPTER 8

It's "Safe" and "Rare"?

I t's one thing to read the book thus far and disregard the facts. It may not bother you that men are primarily responsible for the rise and legalization of abortion in America. It may not bother you that abortion is a tool in the hands of eugenicists and population control advocates. And it may not even bother you to concede that sexually active males use abortion as a "get out of jail free" card, even though women are left to deal with the pregnancy, the surgical or chemical abortion procedure, and the aftermath of abortion.

After all, abortion is a woman's right. Who can tell a woman what to do with her body?

If you refuse to concede that abortion is a means for men to exploit women for their own gain and instead choose to celebrate the right to abort, then you'll need to come to grips with the effects of abortion on women. You are celebrating a right that does tremendous emotional and physical damage to the female gender.

To understand the impact of abortion on women, let's take a look at how and why women abort. Though we often hear about abortion being used in cases of rape and incest, the overwhelming majority of cases are for far more typical reasons.

BIRTH CONTROL

Abortion is the final form of birth control in America. It's used as such for several reasons—primarily because contraceptives are terribly ineffective or, perhaps more likely, Americans aren't using them properly and with regularity. A person may claim they use contraception, but that doesn't mean they use it as designed and every time they have sex.

Abortion proponents often get upset when I link abortion to birth control, but it isn't actually my conclusion. According to a 2010 CDC report, contraceptive use is almost universal among women of childbearing age in America.[223] However, contraception isn't working too well. The Guttmacher Institute reports that one-half of all pregnancies in the U.S. are unintended.

If we agree that most people are using some form of contraception, and since there are over 5.2 million pregnancies each year, that means contraception (whether because of a faulty product or a faulty user) is failing 2.6 million times each year.

And the success rate of contraception hasn't been improving. The U.S. Department of Health and Human Services reports the average probability of an unintended pregnancy in 12 months of contraceptive use in the U.S. is 12 percent. That number hasn't moved since 1995.[224]

Guttmacher Institute researchers Lawrence Finer and Mia Zolna report, "Nearly half of pregnancies among American women are unintended, and about four in 10 of these are terminated by abortion."[225] If contraceptives are failing at least 2.6 million times a year, and roughly half of those unintended pregnancies are ending in abortion, abortion is being used as a final form of birth control.

Pro-abortion advocates get upset because they think this implies that women are unfeeling. They maintain that women wrestle with the decision to abort. I'm not claiming that abortion isn't a hard decision or that women are somehow callous and unfeeling.

I am saying the data doesn't lie.

Fully 75 percent of women having abortions offer convenience-related reasons for doing so. If we carefully review Guttmacher's statements below, we see abortion is a means of birth control:

> The reasons women give for having an abortion underscore their understanding of the responsibilities of parenthood and family life. Three-fourths of women cite concern for or responsibility to other individuals; three-fourths say they cannot afford a child; three-fourths say that having a baby would interfere with work, school or the ability to care for dependents; and half say they do not want to be a single parent or are having problems with their husband or partner.[226]

If we wade through the spin in that paragraph, we note that the primary reasons listed are finances, interference with work or other responsibilities, or issues with the father of the baby. In fact, the primary reasons given may well be the same reasons we would use for preventative contraception.

In a debate, Ann Furedi, the chief executive of BPAS, Britain's largest abortion provider, said, "In the real world, out of women who are using the pill well, about 8 in every 100 will get pregnant in the course of a year.... We need abortion as a backup to contraception."[227]

And that is exactly what abortion is in America today. The backup to, and final form of, birth control.

So is this form of birth control safe for women? Do they suffer any ill effects that should be known and disclosed? How about other family members—do they experience any negative impact when an abortion is performed?

HARMFUL EFFECTS ON WOMEN: DEATH

If abortion is being used primarily as birth control, then is it also saving their lives? If we are going to talk about the harmful effects of abortion on women, is death a primary risk?

It is worth remembering that the original push for the legalization of abortion was to make sure the procedure was safe for women. Our nation was concerned about women's health and wanted to stop back-alley abortions. So, in order to make sure abortion would be "safe" and "rare," it was legalized.

However there weren't enough deaths of mothers by abortion to legitimize the claim that abortion had to be made legal. So facts were fabricated.

Bernard Nathanson wrote, "There were perhaps three hundred or so deaths from criminal abortions annually in the United States in the sixties, but NARAL in its press releases claimed to have data that supported a figure of five thousand."[228]

The claim of 8,000 to 10,000 abortion-related maternal deaths annually was first introduced in 1936 by abortion legalization advocate Dr. Frederick Taussig, who later acknowledged those numbers were based on "the wildest estimates."[229] Dr. Christopher Tietze, an abortion legalization advocate who served as a statistician for Planned Parenthood, dismissed the exaggerated numbers in a 1969 *Scientific American* article:

> Some 30 years ago it was judged that such deaths (from illegal abortion) might number 5,000 to 10,000 per year, but this rate even if it was approximately correct at the time, cannot be anywhere near the true rate now. The total number of deaths from all causes among women of reproductive age in the U.S. is not more than about 50,000 per year. The National Center for Health Statistics listed 235 deaths from abortion in 1965. Total mortality from illegal abortions was undoubtedly larger than that figure, but in all likelihood it was under 1,000.[230]

Others had presumed that abortion was not immediately physically dangerous to women. Dr. Mary Calderone, then medical director of Planned Parenthood, wrote an article in 1960 for the *American Journal of Public Health*, stating, "Abortion, whether therapeutic or illegal, is in the main no longer dangerous, because it is being done well by physicians."[231]

Her conclusion was not just her own. She was citing the judgment reached by 43 medical professionals, who gathered together in a series of eight, three-hour sessions to "exhaustively" address the issue of illegal abortion. According to Calderone, citing the conference of professionals:

> Abortion is no longer a dangerous procedure. This applies not just to therapeutic abortions as performed in hospitals but also to so-called illegal abortions as done by physicians. In 1957 there were only 260 deaths in the whole country attributed to abortions of any kind.[232]

This number of abortion deaths had plummeted by 1972 when, according to the CDC, there were 39 maternal deaths due to illegal abortion and 24 deaths due to legal abortion.[233] That's an 85 percent decline in the 15 years between 1957 and 1972.

So, in 1972 there were a reported 63 deaths due to botched abortions—legal or illegal. While these deaths are tragic, exponentially more people are killed in traffic accidents each year. In 2009, 93 people died on roads in America every day.[234]

Even though the reported number of maternal deaths by abortion was fabricated, and the number of deaths remains small, it is still a viable risk.

The CDC reported that in 2008, the most recent year for which data were available, 12 women died as a result of complications from abortions.[235] And maternal death from legal abortion still happens.

A 24-year-old woman died after a Chicago Planned Parenthood abortionist botched the abortion of her 16-week-old baby on July 20, 2012. The woman suffered severe bleeding from the incomplete abortion but was not transported to a hospital for five-and-a-half hours. The autopsy report indicates fetal parts left behind by Planned Parenthood, a 3/16 inch uterine perforation, and an "extensive" perforation, which may have severed an artery and caused massive internal bleeding. There were 1-1.5 liters of blood in her abdominal cavity, indicating she lost up to 30 percent of her total blood supply.[236]

Another woman died in Maryland on February 7, 2013, after she sought an abortion at 33 weeks from late-term abortionist Dr.

LeRoy Carhart. Jennifer Morbelli, a 29-year-old married kindergarten teacher, first arrived at the Germantown Reproductive Health Center in Germantown, Maryland, on Sunday, February 3. According to a report from Operation Rescue,

> she was seen by pro-life activists [outside the abortion facility] every day through Wednesday. Witnesses said she appeared "pale and weak." Early Thursday morning, the woman began suffering chest pain and other discomforts. Her attempts to reach Carhart were unsuccessful. The woman was taken by her family from her hotel to a nearby hospital emergency room at approximately 5:00 a.m. Efforts by hospital staff to contact Carhart or get informational assistance from the abortion clinic were unsuccessful.
>
> The patient suffered massive internal bleeding into her abdominal cavity. She slipped into a Code Blue condition approximately six times before finally succumbing to her injuries at around 9:30 a.m. The case has been placed with the Medical Examiner for further investigation.[237]

And, as noted above, the leading cause of death for pregnant women is murder. The risk to the mother and child is not just in the abortion clinic; it extends in some cases to a violent male in the mother's life who does not wish her to have the baby.

BOTCHED ABORTIONS

Botched abortions and cruel abortionists can be brutally harmful to women.

Former Philadelphia abortionist Kermit Gosnell, who was convicted for murder in the deaths of infants aborted alive and killed by a scissor snip to their spinal columns, treated his patients with contempt and cruelty. When Davida Johnson changed her mind, he forced her to have an abortion anyway. "I said, 'I don't want to do this,' and he smacked me," Johnson told the Associated Press. "They tied my hands and arms down and gave me more medication."[238]

Another woman was left unattended for hours after Gosnell cut both her cervix and colon in an unsuccessful attempt to remove her baby. Relatives of the woman, who were at first refused entry into Gosnell's clinic, later found her dazed and bleeding and took her to a hospital, where doctors removed a half-foot of her intestine.[239]

A 40-year-old woman is suing a Colorado Planned Parenthood office after the abortionist there forced her to undergo an abortion without anesthesia and left parts of her baby's dismembered body inside her uterus. The woman, who had to be treated in an emergency room, alleges in her lawsuit that she changed her mind while on the operating table because the agreed-upon anesthesia was not administered due to difficulty inserting an I.V. into her vein. The abortionist told her it was too late to change her mind and flipped on the vacuum machine to do the abortion, forcing her to endure the full pain of the seven-minute procedure.[240]

A Michigan woman had to be rushed by ambulance to a hospital in 2009 to stop uncontrolled bleeding six months after her abortion. "If my boyfriend hadn't woken me up that night, I just feel like I could have bled to death in my sleep," said the woman, who was given two units of blood and an emergency D&C. The woman recalled "being in a lot of pain" during the abortion procedure and said she visited the clinic's bathroom after the abortion, where she saw "blood all over the restroom, including on the toilet seat."[241] The local fire department shut down the clinic on December 27, 2012, one day after discovering conditions "dangerous to human life or the public welfare." An inspection revealed, for example, "blood dripping from a sink p-trap in a room used by patients."[242]

Mark Crutcher lists these examples of how women suffer at the hands of abusive abortionists in his exposé of the abortion industry, *Lime 5*:

In response to a woman's screams of pain during her abortion, a clinic worker stuffed a tampon in her mouth. During the procedure, she was so badly injured that she lost all of her reproductive organs and spleen and ended up with a colostomy, as well as permanent damage to her heart, lungs, and kidneys.

An abortionist showed a 12-week-old fetus that he had just aborted to the patient, threw his glove on the floor, and asked her if she was "satisfied."

A woman claimed that her abortionist "ordered [her] on the table and threw her legs apart." She said she felt like she was some animal at which the doctor was irritated.[243]

OTHER PHYSICAL EFFECTS

Other increased physical risks to the mother include cervical, ovarian, and liver cancers; uterine perforations; cervical lacerations; pre-term deliveries and other labor complications; and pelvic inflammatory disease, or PID, an infection of the uterus that can damage the Fallopian tubes.[244]

Another physical risk garnering debate in the media is the increased risk of breast cancer after an abortion. Despite denying a link between abortion and breast cancer, a 2009 study published in the journal, *Cancer Epidemiology, Biomarkers and Prevention*, found

...examined risk factors were consistent with the effects of previous studies on younger women. Specifically, older age, family history of breast cancer, earlier menarche age, induced abortion, and oral contraceptives were associated with an increased risk of breast cancer.[245]

More recently, Dr. Angela Lanfranchi, president of the Breast Cancer Prevention Institute, reported at a National Press Club media briefing that "there are 70 published studies examining the risk of induced abortion and breast cancer of which 55 show a positive correlation and 33 are statistically significant."[246] According to Lanfranchi, "The overwhelming evidence from worldwide epidemiologic studies shows that abortion is a cause for breast cancer."[247]

IMPACT ON SUBSEQUENT CHILDREN

Abortion also presents potential risks to subsequent children who are not aborted.

Dr. Freda McKissic Bush, an obstetrician-gynecologist and president/CEO of the Medical Institute for Sexual Health, states, "Abortion greatly increases a woman's chance of giving birth prematurely in the next pregnancy."[248] The rate of prematurity, which is the leading cause of infant death in the U.S., has doubled since the legalization of abortion, Dr. Bush reports, rising from six percent before 1970 to 12.8 percent in 2006 and currently at 11.7 percent.

Prematurity is a problem that disproportionately impacts African-American women, says Dr. Bush. Black women have premature babies, before 32 weeks gestation, at three times the rate of white women. This fact points to abortion, since black women have 35 percent of all abortions but blacks make up just 13 percent of the population.

"There are over 130 studies in the medical literature showing that abortion leads to an increase in very premature births (births before 8 months of pregnancy)," according to Dr. Bush. "Those preemie babies are the ones who end up with cerebral palsy, developmental problems and mental impairments."[249]

A Finnish study found an increased risk of pre-term birth after abortion and reported that the risk increases with two or more abortions. Dr. Reija Klemetti, who led the research, said that "for every 1000 women, three who have had no abortion will have a baby born under 28 weeks.... This rises to four women among those who have had one abortion, six women who have had two abortions, and 11 women who have had three or more."[250]

Abortion activist and NARAL cofounder Lawrence Lader believed abortion would ultimately be beneficial to society. Writing in *The Humanist* magazine, Lader predicted the positive effects of abortion:

> The impact of the abortion revolution may be too vast to assess immediately. It should usher in an era when every child will be

wanted, loved, and properly cared for; when the incidence of infanticides and battered children should be sharply reduced.[251]

Yet violence breeds violence. One violent act of abortion (which may or may not be preceded by other violence) can now be connected to higher incidences of further violence.

A 2005 study led by Dr. Priscilla Coleman found, "Compared to women with no history of induced abortion, those with one prior abortion had a 144 percent higher risk for child physical abuse."[252] Dr. Michael J. New, an assistant professor at the University of Michigan-Dearborn, cites data from the U.S. Statistical Abstract showing that child abuse increased by 400 percent between 1973 and 1990.[253] A recent study found that serious child abuse injuries involving hospitalization rose 4.9 percent between 1997 and 2009.[254]

Abortion advocates claim that wanted children will be welcomed and loved while those born from unplanned pregnancies are more likely to suffer abuse, but empirical research contradicts that view. A 1980 study of 674 abused children conducted by researcher Edward Lenoski found that 91 percent of the abused children in the study were wanted by their parents.[255] What makes this striking is that just half of all pregnancies in the U.S. are planned, according to the Guttmacher Institute. This means that abused children are disproportionately from families where the parents wanted and planned for them.

The logic of abortion—which makes unborn children expendable and subject to death—also puts born children at risk. Psychiatrist Philip Ney suggests the following seven mechanisms explain why abortion makes child abuse more likely:

- Abortion decreases an individual's instinctual restraint against the occasional rage felt toward those dependent on his or her care.
- Permissive abortion diminishes the taboo against aggressing [against] the defenseless.
- Abortion increases the hostility between the generations.

- Abortion has devalued children, thus diminishing the value of caring for children.
- Abortion increases guilt and self-hatred, which the parent takes out on the child.
- Abortion increases hostile frustration, intensifying the battle of the sexes, for which children are scapegoated.
- Abortion truncates the developing mother-infant bond, thereby diminishing her future mothering capability.[256] [257]

Instead of incidences of battered children being sharply reduced, as Lader predicted, abortion has brought further violence to children both inside and outside the womb.

PSYCHOLOGICAL IMPACTS

Novelist Erica Jong supports abortion but is candid about its emotional toll. The author of provocative, sexual novels writes that abortion, for her, was too high a price to pay:

> As a seventeen-year-old freshman at Barnard, I got my first diaphragm from Planned Parenthood (a college tradition). I never got pregnant accidentally because I knew that an abortion would make me terribly sad. I loved children, dogs, cats and other living things, and I understood that terminating a pregnancy would be extremely hard for me emotionally.[258]

Research confirms what Jong understood: the mental health consequences of abortion are enormous. A 1997 Finnish study found, according to a review of its results, that "women who abort are approximately four times more likely to die in the following year than women who carry their pregnancies to term."[259] Relative to women who did give birth, women who aborted a year prior to their death were:

- seven times more likely to die of suicide,
- four times more likely to die of injuries related to accidents, and

- 14 times more likely to die from homicide. [260]

Researchers believe the greater frequency of death from accidents and homicide may be linked to higher rates of suicidal or risk-taking behavior. An Elliot Institute review of the study suggests "that induced abortion produces an unnatural physical and psychological stress on women that can result in a negative impact on their general health."[261] And, in some cases, death.

A 2011 study published in the *British Journal of Psychiatry* reviewed data from 22 published studies and found a link between abortion and mental health difficulties. The meta-analysis of studies looked at 877,181 participants, of whom 163,831 had undergone an abortion, finding, "Women who had undergone an abortion experienced an 81 percent increased risk of mental health problems."[262]

The study found increased risks of the following separate mental health effects for women who had abortions:

- anxiety disorders (34 percent),
- depression (37 percent),
- alcohol use/abuse (110 percent),
- marijuana use/abuse (220 percent), and
- suicide behaviors (155 percent). [263]

In addition to the research above, post-abortion effects researcher Dr. David Reardon reports that at least 21 studies show a link between abortion and substance abuse.[264]

A 2003 study from Reardon's Elliot Institute found that women having abortions were 160 percent more likely to seek psychiatric care in the 90 days afterwards than were women who had delivered their children. The study, published in the *Canadian Medical Association Journal*, reviewed the medical records of 56,741 California Medicaid patients and found that the frequency of psychiatric treatment was significantly higher for at least four years following abortion.[265]

Dr. Bryan C. Calhoun, professor and Vice-Chair of the Department of Obstetrics and Gynecology at West Virginia University-Charleston, says the side effects of abortion are broad ranging and inevitable:

As certain as the effect of the law of gravity on a person who jumps from a bridge, so are the certainty of the effects that we've seen on women's health on the person who violates the moral law in taking an innocent life.

Calhoun says over the last 40 years abortion has been a health disaster for women and a public health disaster in the U.S., which costs the nation more than $1.2 billion annually. [266]

It also takes its toll on close family members.

IMPACT ON OTHER FAMILY MEMBERS

While women are greatly impacted physically and emotionally by abortion, other family members are negatively impacted, as well. In what has become known as PASS (post-abortion survivor syndrome), the siblings of aborted babies may deal with very difficult emotional struggles.

It is likely that around 50 percent of younger Americans have aborted siblings. If and when the surviving children come to the knowledge they were chosen to live, while their siblings were not, they may wrestle with very difficult questions.

"The most prominent symptom of PASS is existential guilt, 'I feel I don't deserve to be alive,'" says Dr. Philip Ney, head of the Department of Psychiatry at Royal Jubilee Hospital in Canada.

"Other symptoms include pervasive anxiety, fear of the future, sense of impending doom, self-injury, obsessive thinking, poor self-identity, low self-esteem, self-destructive behavior, fear of becoming psychotic and dissociation." [267]

PASS may start at a very young age, and the child doesn't even necessarily have to be told of the previous abortion(s). "There is increasing evidence that even very young children may be aware of maternal abortions despite family attempts to maintain secrecy," according to a 1984 study. The study found that a five-year-old girl's "withdrawn regression was related to her mother's multiple abortions and her own fear of being destroyed through maternal aggression."[268]

ABORTION'S IMPACT ON MEN

While this book's main purpose is to properly show abortion for what it is—the exploitation of women and children at the hands of men—not all men are exploiting women. Men often experience negative and harmful effects from abortion, whether they wanted the abortion or not.

That's the verdict of the little research that has been conducted on this issue. The scarcity of scientific investigation into abortion's effects on men is probably because society regards abortion as a women's issue. It's something that, supposedly, is of no consequence to men. But the reality is exactly opposite. After all, even miscarriage takes its toll on men and "results in higher 'difficulty coping' and 'despair' scores on the Perinatal Grief Scale" than for women, according to a 2007 review of reports about abortion's impact on men.[269]

That review examined the limited studies conducted between 1973 and 2006 and found a few common themes. "At the least," researcher Dr. Catharine T. Coyle summarized, men:

> struggle with ambivalence both before and after abortion. While abortion seems to bring a sense of relief, other emotions including anxiety, grief, guilt, and powerlessness are also reported consequent to abortion.

Coyle also noted a "tendency among men to defer the abortion decision to their female partners as well as a tendency to repress their own emotions in an attempt to support their partners."[270]

In a subsequent review of the psychological effects of abortion on men, Coyle concluded, "Men may suffer intense grief after abortion as well as regret, helplessness, guilt, anxiety, anger, and emasculation." The abortion experience may be so profound as to cause post-traumatic stress disorder and lead men to self-medicate using controlled substances. The range of symptoms experienced by post-abortive men, Coyle explains, may include "anxiety, persistent thoughts about the lost child, difficulty concentrating, sleep disturbances, and other somatic complaints such as headaches or palpitations."[271]

With 55 million abortions performed in America since 1973, millions of men have been party, willing or unwilling, to an abortion decision. More and more men are going public with their own pain and suffering caused by abortion. Their words are heartrending.

A married father of two who, with his wife's agreement, aborted their third child:

> Hardly a day goes by that I don't shudder and almost weep again for the murder I helped to bring about. Quite often I even wake up in the morning thinking painfully of the undeniably selfish act I did over 11 years ago—STILL! I know I overrode in my core being my conscience (dulled at the time) and my Fatherhood instinct. No two ways about it: I acted—no, I was a coward. My action, despite my confession and repentance before my Creator—continues to rob much of the joy from my life.[272]

A man, who at 17 convinced his girlfriend to have an abortion, looks at the experience 24 years later:

> It's amazing to think that back then we thought our lives would be ruined with the birth of a baby. Twenty-four years later, we both know that our lives would have been significantly better if we had kept the child. Twenty-four years of pain and suffering could have been avoided if we had just dealt with a few months of disappointing friends and family. The true friends and family would have eventually come around and supported us—we know that now. We could have had our daughter, who would be

graduating college by now. We would not have gone through the depression and struggles that we did.

If we only kept the baby.... [273]

A good friend shared his own hard and painful journey after multiple abortions in this account:

By my mid-twenties, I had been a part of three unplanned pregnancies with three different women. All three women wanted abortions, and I was more than happy to pay for all three. Back then all my thoughts were completely self-centered, and a child was not in the plans. I can remember feeling a small amount of guilt, mainly because these women had to undergo a very unpleasant procedure. And I knew, deep down, that abortion was wrong, but I quickly and easily got over it and moved on with my life.

Years later, I had gotten married and, during my second year of marriage, became a Christian. My eyes had been opened to all my sins. The three abortions weighed heavily on my heart, and I asked for forgiveness from Jesus Christ. I knew I was forgiven, and I felt His forgiveness! I remember thinking, all of my repressed guilt was gone, and I'll never have to deal with abortion again.

A year later, my beautiful daughter was born, and I was the happiest dad on earth. Then, six months later, my wife comes to me late on a Friday night and says, "I'm pregnant again, but I don't want another baby, and I have an abortion scheduled first thing Monday morning."

I almost passed out from the shock. I tried like crazy to talk her out of it, but there was no stopping her. I offered to take my daughter and the baby and relieve her of any responsibility. Nothing changed her mind, and she went through with it, as planned. My heart was crushed; this was pain I had never felt.

Our family was broken and torn apart by this abortion; she left me, and we eventually divorced.

The only way I made it through that time was through my faith. I have only ever told two people about this experience until recently. I was able, through the power of Jesus Christ, to forgive my former wife, and hope one day she can experience His forgiveness, as well.

The pain from that abortion will always be with me. But then I have to say a prayer and give all my pain to Jesus, or it just becomes too much.[274]

Whether by action or inaction, the man who allows or approves of abortion will suffer. Indeed, he creates a void in the relationship with the mother and, possibly, other family members. Post-abortion researcher Dr. Vincent Rue describes multiple ways that abortion drives a wedge between partners, leading to isolation or dysfunctional communication patterns. These effects include:

- a reduction in self-disclosures by both partners, which decreases the intimacy necessary for relationship survival;
- increased use of defensive communication behaviors (e.g., interpersonal hostility);
- the development of partner communication apprehensiveness (fear translated into avoidance behaviors), the erosion of trust, and the evolution into a closed system of interaction, as opposed to an open and dynamic one; and
- a loss of spiritual connectedness to God and to one's partner with the advent of guilt, shame, and isolation.[275]

Pope John Paul II commented on the consequence of the absent male in the abortion decision and the impact on family connections: "[I]n this way the family is thus mortally wounded and profaned in its nature as a community of love and in its vocation to be the 'sanctuary of life.'"[276]

Abortion has no winners. Women are emotionally torn, often experiencing years of negative and crushing symptoms. It is becoming clearer that men are also torn, though their symptoms may exhibit in other ways, including violence against themselves and other people, as well as stress syndromes. And the baby loses her life.

We celebrate abortion as a right, but it is, in more ways than one, killing our families.

MEN CAN
END IT

CHAPTER 9

THE MAN VOID

Though I know both men and women are reading this book, the next two chapters are addressed specifically to my Y chromosome brothers.

Women, feel free to read on. I hope you find the information and perspective helpful.

In this chapter, we'll look briefly at the decline of the American male and how it has impacted (or not impacted) abortion. In the next chapter, I'll outline how men must take action if we are to save our families, communities, and nation from the horror of abortion.

Men, I'm going to be very candid with you. There are too many dead humans, destroyed women, and wrecked families lying in our wake to mince words.

Men in America have failed our nation. I put myself in that same category, so my words are for all of us.

In order to properly understand the abortion epidemic in our culture today, we must have the courage to look at ourselves. Abortion exists because of us. It is promoted because of us. It is still around because of us. And the blood of 55 million babies is on our hands, as is the havoc and harm brought to women and families for over a generation.

Whether or not you are a post-abortive man, you must confront the reality of abortion in America.

WHERE ARE THE REAL MEN?

While Planned Parenthood enjoys a $1 billion budget, the sum total budget of the largest life-affirming groups in the country is around $30 million. The monetary effort to end abortion is a small fraction of the monetary effort to continue it.

Yet Americans spend over $13 billion on porn every year.[277] Most of those dollars, guys, are coming out of our pockets. We make plenty of room in our budgets for porn, alcohol, and other self-pleasures, but we can't seem to find money, time, or resources to rescue babies and families from abortion.

We have become a self-indulgent, undisciplined, reckless, self-pleasing generation of men. We have forgotten our place in society, and we allow the termination of a human life once every 25 seconds because of it. We repeat Adam's behavior time and again, avoiding responsibility for our sexual behaviors, our marriages, our families, our communities, and our nation. But we can quote statistics about sports and dark beer like geniuses.

The harshest judgment and criticism in America regarding abortion should be directed at men who treat it as a "women's issue."

Abortion is not a women's issue. It is a parental issue. Our consistent denial of such is the greatest blight on what is becoming a pathetic and numb gender in America. The war for unborn babies is, by and large, being fought by women. There are precious few men who have committed themselves to ending abortion. Most life-affirming women working to stop abortion in America are largely unaided by the ones who impregnate females and use abortion as birth control to satisfy their sexual appetites.

If men *en masse* had the backbone to enter the fray and defend the weakest among us, who knows how much progress could be made towards protecting both the children and their mothers? Indeed, our neglect and ignorance of the thousands of pre-born children who are killed every day in America is the severest indictment on men who claim to love God, their wives, children, and communities.

We are the worst of hypocrites.

We like the fact that abortion has become a "women's issue." By placing all of the blame and responsibility on them for making an "informed choice," we wash our hands of responsibility and continue on our selfish way.

American men today have unbridled sexual appetites. Due to our sexually saturated culture, we can now have sex with any number of women on a regular basis. The idea of a monogamous relationship has become "old fashioned" and "traditional." So those of us who feel enlightened enjoy years of sexual freedom, moving from partner to partner when we choose, all in the name of progress.

Pregnancy, however, represents some things many men don't like. First, it means we may not get as much sex. Pregnant women may not want to have sex often, especially as pregnancy progresses. After birth, a child interrupts our sexual lifestyle. A crying baby in the middle of the night, changing diapers, and the sheer emotional force of being a parent can ruin libido. The child becomes the focus, not our sexual pleasure.

Second, pregnancy means responsibility. Now our female companion may need us to stick around and pay some bills. During pregnancy, she will be talking about cribs, baby clothes, formula, and diapers. Those things cost money and can add up quickly. Spending money on babies means less money for video games, pornography, fantasy football, and beer.

Third, pregnancy means permanence. If we commit to the child, we may need to commit to the mother. That wasn't in the plan. We are fine committing to the mother as long as we get what we want, but we like to have a back-out plan if need be. A baby? A baby means we could get locked in for life. That's not in the cards.

It would be perfect if she could get an abortion. It's quick, it's easy, and we don't have to do anything except pay for it (maybe). She'll no longer be pregnant, and we can get back to a carefree, sex-centered lifestyle.

But we really don't want this on our consciences. We would rather this be a woman thing. If abortion were a female issue, we wouldn't have to deal with the pangs of guilt.

Good news. Abortion is a women's issue.

We don't even have to tell her we want her to get an abortion. All she has to do is ask what we think. And we now have the opportunity to utter those famous words, "It's your decision. I'll support you in whatever you decide."

Which is the same as saying, "Go ahead and abort my child. I don't care enough about you or the baby to protect either one of you."

Plus, we already know what she will decide when we leave the decision up to her. We are removing any real security we could be providing as a man and, instead, placing the entire burden of the decision and responsibility for the child on her. She will most likely have an abortion out of panic because she realizes we aren't committed to her or the child.

It's no wonder we've made abortion a women's issue. It gives us the right to exercise our lifestyle without consequence, and we get to be a proponent of women's rights at the same time.

We satisfy our self-indulgent lusts by spending billions of dollars on sexual appetites, while 3,500 pre-born children die daily in America.

I now believe a large majority of men have bought the lie the media has been selling for years. We are stupid, immature, weak people who should be thankful we have a woman around to keep us from destroying ourselves.

A generation of man-degrading media has taught us the following:

- Men are unable to control their impulses.
- Men are incapable of leading their families or their communities.
- Men are dumber than women.
- Men have no right to comment or engage in women's issues.

The culture has successfully convinced men, in general, that we have no voice on many issues. Even if we did, we have no right to speak out.

THE ABSENT CHURCH

As with most challenges in America today, the social and moral ills that impact society are the same inside and outside the Church. Despite overwhelming Biblical evidence that we are to affirm innocent human life and protect it, many denominations have caved into social pressure and won't defend innocent, unborn life.

Consider this statement from the United Methodist Church:

> Our belief in the sanctity of unborn human life makes us reluctant to approve abortion. But we are equally bound to respect the sacredness of the life and well-being of the mother and the unborn child. We recognize tragic conflicts of life with life that may justify abortion, and in such cases we support the legal option of abortion under proper medical procedures by certified medical providers.[278]

The statement is both confounding and conflicting. The United Methodist Church upholds the sanctity of human life while, at the same time, inexplicably upholding abortion in cases of the "life and well-being of the mother." If it referred to those rarest of situations where the life of the mother is actually threatened because of the pregnancy, that would be worth discussing. That minuscule number of situations is, indeed, tragic.

However, the statement also mentions "well-being," which could mean any number of things, none of which include the possibility of death. "Well-being" might refer to financial challenge, emotional distress, or the fact she'll gain weight through pregnancy. Who knows?

The statement, purposefully ambiguous, leaves room for all sorts of interpretations, thus showing that the United Methodist Church is a pro-abortion denomination. A number of other churches, supposedly holding to Christian doctrine, claim to be in favor of abortion.

Though the following article appeared some 15 years ago, it holds true today. *World* magazine, in a piece called "Silence of the Shepherds," documented the silence of ministers on the issue of abortion using three methods.[279]

First, it asked 20 well-known Christian leaders to provide a full sermon they had preached on the topic of abortion. Only six of the 20 were able to do so. Just three more supplied a sermon excerpt that addressed abortion.

Second, it used the results of a study conducted by a Regent University student for her master's thesis. She surveyed 104 pastors from evangelical, charismatic, mainline, and fundamentalist churches in the South Hampton Roads area of Virginia. Seventy-six percent of pastors agreed that life begins at conception. Sixty-nine percent said the church should speak out on abortion. Just 39 percent said they had preached a full sermon on abortion. Evangelical ministers had the highest percentage of sermons preached on abortion (58 percent).

The conclusion of Regent student Molly Stone: "The average clergyman does not actively encourage his church to be involved in pro-life activity." She observed, "Even actions that clergy say are highly acceptable are typically not performed." While 70 percent of these ministers said crisis pregnancy centers were their preferred pro-life organization, the same number said they did not support a CPC.

According to *World* editor Marvin Olasky, "Only a third ever encouraged walking in a march for life or ever showed a pro-life film. Only one-sixth had endorsed pickets or prayer at abortion clinics. Rescues had been encouraged by 7 percent."

Third, *World* asked ten well-known pro-life leaders to comment on church involvement. They were unanimous that the church is AWOL on this issue. Dr. John Willke, who helped found the modern American pro-life movement in the late 1960s, said the silence of America's churches is "deadly" and widespread: "You see it in every denomination."

Frederica Matthewes Green understands the silence of the church. "From the point of view of movement activists, the response of the church has ranged from weak to wimpy," she writes. "Denominations may have grand anti-abortion statements on the books, but active support for the cause, especially at the local level, seems scant."[280]

Indeed, the problem may well be both a cause and effect. Pastors and priests may be reluctant to address abortion in church because there are so many people in church who are getting abortions. Because they don't address it, people may not understand what abortion is and the harmful impacts. So they abort. Then the church is in the awkward position of potentially alienating parishioners who are post-abortive. It's a vicious cycle that only ends in death and sadness.

And abortion is frequent and customary inside the church. The Guttmacher Institute reports that fully 65 percent of women who get abortions claim to be Protestant (37 percent) or Catholic (28 percent). Some 20 percent of the women who claim Christianity identify themselves as "born-again," and 15 percent of women having abortions attend a religious service once or more a week.[281]

Why is the Church so ineffective when it comes to dealing with abortion? Why are abortions virtually as prevalent inside the Church as outside?

Because men are failing our churches.

MEN BEING MEN ... OR WOMEN

Since 85 percent of abortions are performed on unwed mothers, it is obvious that men are failing to promote and establish marriage in its proper context.

The public debate over marriage is one I don't wish to repeat here. Regardless of your view on marriage, there are two truths about marriage that are inescapable:

- Marriage provides boundaries for man's sexuality.
- Marriage provides the framework of security for having and raising children.

When a man and woman take the vows of marriage, they are agreeing to remain sexually committed to one another and to remain together for the sake of the couple and children.

Those oaths are broken on a ridiculously regular basis. But the problem isn't the covenant and institution of marriage. The problem is the people getting married. Men have lost their way when it comes to marriage. Mark Driscoll, an outspoken pastor in Seattle, and the author, with his wife, Grace, of *Real Marriage*, accurately notes that American culture is filled with "boys who can shave." These are grown men who refuse to take on their God-given masculine responsibilities and live in a permanent state of adolescence. Instead of shouldering the weight of manhood during their twenties, they subsist in a series of dead-end jobs, live with their parents, or take up with girlfriends, enjoying the privileges of marriage without any of its obligations.

Census Bureau data sheds light on this. In 1960, the median age of first marriage for men was 22.8, climbing to 28.6 by 2012. But another measure illustrates the so-called Peter Pan syndrome much more starkly. Sociologists link the transition to adulthood with five distinct phases: finishing school, leaving home, financial self-sufficiency, marriage, and parenthood. In 1960, 65 percent of men[282] had made it past all five mileposts by age 30. Just one-third of 30-year-old men had done so in 2000.[283]

Without letting men off the hook, it's true that one factor in all this is feminism, which has altered traditional roles and, in some cases, led men to say, "No," to marriage. Just 29 percent of men ages 18-34 say a good marriage is one of the most important things in their life.[284] If men, who are becoming increasingly selfish and self-pleasing, can have their sexual appetites fed outside the boundaries of marriage, can control their finances without "investing" in the normal aspects of a committed relationship with a female, and can avoid having children for as long as possible, why get married at all?

While 20th century feminism has benefits, it also has drawbacks. Writing in *The Atlantic* in 2010, Hanna Rosin, author of *The End of Men*, chronicles male decline and the rise of women:

Man has been the dominant sex since, well, the dawn of mankind. But for the first time in human history, that is changing—and with shocking speed.... Earlier this year, for the first time in American history, the balance of the workforce tipped toward women, who now hold a majority of the nation's jobs. The working class, which has long defined our notions of masculinity, is slowly turning into a matriarchy, with men increasingly absent from the home and women making all the decisions. Women dominate today's colleges and professional schools—for every two men who will receive a B.A. this year, three women will do the same. Of the 15 job categories projected to grow the most in the next decade in the U.S., all but two are occupied primarily by women.[285]

Where, then, are the men?

Becoming increasingly feminized, it appears.

The media has overwhelmingly promoted the idea of stronger females and weaker men. S.T. Karnick writes about the pilot episode of a since-cancelled sitcom, *Big Shots*, in which a divorced man announces: "Men—we're the new women." Karnick observes,

> [T]he war against boys seems to have created three main character patterns for the adult male of our time: sensitive guys who want to please women; weenies and dorks who want only to be left alone to drink beer and play video games with their dork buddies; and thugs who, in rebellion against their unnatural education, are perpetually concerned with proving their toughness through increasingly loutish behavior. There are, of course, examples of decent, positively masculine males in the culture, but they are becoming increasingly overwhelmed by the products of educational and cultural feminization.[286]

Quick—try to think of a TV sitcom in recent years where the father or main leading man wasn't a weak-willed moron. *Everybody Loves Raymond? King of Queens? Two and a Half Men? The Simpsons? American Dad?*

Another reader of Karnick's article conceded he was "hard-pressed to come up with a male figure on TV that possesses strong (traditional) male characteristics and who isn't some sort of bombastic oaf who is all tough and no brains. Where are the Ward Cleavers, Mike Bradys, Cliff Huxtables who used to populate TV?"[287]

Feminism in its modern form has killed other positive aspects of manhood, and men have allowed it to happen. Dr. Laura Schlessinger wryly observed:

Now it is difficult to find a man who values virginity, purity, and innocence when females dress like babes.... [W]ho puts any rational stock in protecting and providing when women have said they can do and be it all without a man? Men now figure they can benefit with less pressure of responsibility and use women to insure the acquisition of more goodies. Who sees any point in sacrificing for what they see are emasculating ball-busters. They think, "Open your own door, get this seat first if you can, get a job so I can relax, you said you're equal, so you pay for dinner, you said you could have/do it all ... so do it!" Chivalry is largely dead and feminism is the murderer.[288]

Men have allowed themselves to be portrayed as oversexed, less-than-intelligent, brutish creatures who cannot get through life without a woman leading them around. And we bought the lie and live it out.

Ironically, even abortion advocates complain about the lack of male involvement. Anne Taylor Fleming once called for greater male involvement in support of abortion rights, stating,

I dare say that many of them have impregnated women along the way, and been let off the hook in a big, big way ... when the women went ahead and had abortions.... [I]t would sure be nice to hear from all those men out there whose lives have been changed, bettered and substantially eased because they were not forced into unwanted fatherhood.[289]

Does our culture even recognize what a compassionate, disciplined, strong, and steady man looks like? Do we recognize men as protectors of their nation and their families? Indeed, the freedom and prosperity we enjoy was secured through the enormous personal sacrifice of the wealth, time, and blood of millions, mostly men.

So why aren't men protecting their own children and the mothers of those children when it comes to abortion?

DO MEN REALLY ACCEPT THE SANCTITY OF LIFE?

We act according to what we believe. This is true about any aspect of life. We are creatures who behave according to our worldview.

In the book, *How Now Shall We Live?* Chuck Colson outlined the three core questions that everyone consciously or unconsciously answers and uses to order their lives:

- Where did we come from, and who are we?
- What has gone wrong with the world?
- What can we do to fix it?

Our core beliefs about who we are, why we are here, and what is wrong with the world dictate in large part how we behave. If we, as men, have a self-centered worldview, we behave in ways that benefit ourselves. If we, as men, have a selfless worldview, we behave in ways that ultimately benefit others.

If we believe in God, we are inclined to behave (or try to behave) in ways that reflect our love and gratitude towards Him. If we don't believe in God, we are inclined to behave in ways that reflect other relative human values. These may include honorable things such as morality, ethics, or community. Or they may reflect baser things such as vengeance, power, or chaos.

Either way, how we act, where we spend our time, and how we invest our money are all reflective of our worldview. We act according to what we believe.

A primary reason men do not rise up and protect the lives and well-being of women and unborn children is we don't really believe in the sanctity of all human life.

If we did believe that every woman has infinite value and that we, as men, should partner with them and give ourselves up for them, we would not consider abortion an option. Abortion exploits women and, as demonstrated, is harmful to their emotional, spiritual, and sometimes physical well-being. Abortion degrades females and widens the gender gap. It ultimately empowers men and demeans women.

If we did believe that every woman has infinite value and that we, as men, should partner with them and give ourselves up for them, we would not be hooked on porn, having affairs, and moving from sexual partner to sexual partner. These all destroy relationships, deter commitment, and breed insecurity.

If we did believe that every conceived human being, whether planned or unplanned, has eternal value and that we, as men, have the honor and privilege of protecting and defending innocent life, we would rise up *en masse* and fight tooth and nail for unborn children. We would not only bring our own sexuality in check so we didn't cause unplanned pregnancies, we would demand the right to protect all innocent human beings. We would decry *Roe v. Wade*—not just on the grounds that it gives complete freedom to willfully terminate unborn life. We would decry it because it prohibits us from protecting those who are dependent on us for shelter and safety.

Why then are men not truly in support of the sanctity of life? The answer lies in our discussion about the first worldview question: Where did we come from, and who are we? The desire and passion to protect unborn life is directly correlated to our answer.

Acknowledging variations, Americans generally fall into one of two camps regarding origin. We were created, or we evolved. Many major world religions claim that a Creator brought the world and humankind to life. A life form higher than ours designed us, gave us life, and put us here.

If this is our belief, we are inclined to believe that this Being had some reason or rationale for creating us. While deists hold to the belief that God created us and then left us alone to grow and develop as a planet, other religions show a God who is intimately involved and working in and through His creation.

Because this Creator is higher and wiser than us, He has a plan for us. And, as men, we concede that the Creator works through us, even when things do not go as we planned here on earth.

Thus, the answer to, "Where did we come from?" for this worldview is, "From the Creator." That knowledge gives value to life and purpose to existence.

If we believe we evolved, without any intervention from a higher being, the value of life is not determined by a being other than us. We value life as we see fit. That valuation may be based on numerous factors including philosophy, culture, social conditions, financial conditions, and so on.

This group of men holds to the belief that the answer to the question, "Where did we come from?" is, "We evolved through no intervention from any other higher being."

The second part of the worldview question and its answer stem naturally from the first part. The person who holds to a Creator of some sort naturally knows that the answer to, "Who are we?" is, "We are created beings, formed by a higher being." The person who believes in evolution answers the "Who are we?" query, "We are evolved beings who came about by chance."

The reason this is vital to man's defense of the unborn is value. Our worldview determines how we value each other and human life in general. If we believe we are created by a higher being, our value is not self-determined. The higher being has the prerogative to assign our value. If we are evolved, the value of human life is defined by us. There is no one above us to answer to, so we can assign value to life as we see fit.

So, the reason many men in America do not actively work to defend innocent human life is because they don't believe we are created by a higher being who has a purpose and plan for life. Instead, many men believe we have evolved, giving us the authority and power to assign value to human life in whatever manner we choose.

There are many examples of male atheists who are life affirming, and I applaud them. They assign value to life on moral or ethical grounds rather than a Creator's decree. The difference is, of course, that value is still assigned by man and can change at will, whereas value assigned by a higher being is not subject to human variables.

Examples of the arbitrary assignment of value abound in world history. Modern slavery is simply the devaluation of one population by another to serve its purposes. Sex trafficking is the devaluation of certain groups of women to serve the purpose of other, typically male, groups. Abortion is the devaluation of human life, based on stage of development, to serve other humans who are farther along in that development.

All of these examples are, of course, discriminatory. Slavery discriminates based on race, sex trafficking is (generally) discrimination based on gender, and abortion involves discrimination based on both race and gender, adding stage of development as another basis for discriminating.

How does abortion discriminate in so many ways? Abortion is rooted in eugenics, which is typically grounded in racial discrimination. Abortion exploits women, so it discriminates along gender lines. And abortion discriminates against a less mature human being, in that the unborn child is not yet mature enough to speak, express herself, or sue the offending party. It also discriminates based on handicap (over 90 percent of pre-born babies diagnosed with Down syndrome in America are aborted).

Ironically, American culture is now repulsed by slavery and sex trafficking. We find racial and gender discrimination distasteful and unacceptable. We have yet to fully understand the more complete discrimination against women and children entailed by abortion.

Men don't necessarily consider their internal beliefs and worldview when advocating abortion (whether actively promoting and engaging in it, or passively ignoring it). However, every man that allows and acknowledges abortion as the right and moral thing to do logically and unmistakably assigns an arbitrary and reduced value to mother and child. We can then conclude a pro-abortion male agrees that we are not created but evolved—and thus can determine our own value.

Or these men do believe in a Creator and ignore or disagree with how value is assigned to human life. Ignorance plays a pivotal role in the cultural application of abortion. Many men who claim to have faith in God are in favor of abortion, but they are so because they either aren't serious about that faith or they haven't studied its tenets, making their religion weak and inarticulate. Then there are men who are life affirming until an unplanned pregnancy happens in their world. A father, a boyfriend, a husband politically supports the life-affirming effort until a pregnancy becomes an inconvenience in his personal life. Conviction is lost, and he becomes a hypocrite—proud to publicly support the defense of unborn life, while privately condoning abortion.

Either way, these men were never serious or committed to the protection of innocent human life and gender equality in the first place.

TEMPTING PHILOSOPHIES

While many men do claim to be life affirming and refuse abortion in their private lives, there are still subtle philosophies that chip away at our resolve.

The major arguments are:

- Abortion is a women's issue.
- Life progresses in value as it matures.
- Abortion is a just and proper means to avoid other social ills, such as overpopulation, abandonment, and financial strain on governments.
- Life-affirming groups just want to save babies and ignore the negative consequences of birth on the family. They want to rescue children from abortion and just care about saving life, not caring for her after birth.
- We should not be focused on abortion—we should be focused on unplanned pregnancy prevention.

1. Abortion is a women's issue. We've dealt with this in great detail. It is only worth noting here to make one other point: Many men who are life affirming genuinely believe there is nothing they can do about the abortion holocaust. Because *Roe v. Wade* took away men's right to protect their own unborn children, and because media and government continue to relentlessly repeat the false idea that abortion is confined to the female gender, these men are inclined to shy away from engaging the issue. They believe they have no power or right to fight for the unborn and true gender equality.

2. Life progresses in value as it matures. Because the abortion community can no longer maintain that life in the womb is a "clump of cells" or "fetal tissue," their argument has evolved. Since medical science has proven beyond reasonable doubt that human life begins at conception, and that the new life is a separate and distinct individual with two parents, abortion now becomes a question of the value of life—not the existence of life itself.

Others have covered this vital point in great detail (see Scott Klusendorf's *The Case for Life*). The progressive valuation approach can seep into the thinking of life-affirming men, eroding a commitment to the unborn and their mothers.

The core idea of progressive valuation is that the child grows in value as she matures. Aborting before the child has reached a certain stage of development is acceptable based on various factors. These may include so-called viability, the ability to feel pain, certain organ development, sentience, etc.

Progressive valuation is a slippery slope and, to the life-affirming man, irrelevant. The life-affirming man recognizes that the unborn child has infinite value at the time she is created and that her value is dependent on what sort of being she is, not on her stage of development (or any other variable factor). In other words, an unborn child is as alive at one week as she is at 40 weeks—and as dead at both stages of development if aborted.

The progressive valuation approach attempts to make a black-and-white issue grey.

There are men who believe abortion prior to a certain stage of development is acceptable. This view is not a life-affirming view; it is an abortion-favoring view. And it is a view that allows man's subjective view of value, based on development, to dictate life and death.

3. Abortion is required to keep other social ills at bay. At Online for Life, I regularly receive emails from well-meaning people who are genuinely concerned about social welfare. I am often asked why we should save babies from abortion when we have so many born children on welfare, in the foster care system, in drug-infested homes, and so forth.

Though I understand and share the concern for children in American society, the underlying premise of the question is disturbing.

The premise is: it is better to take the lives of unborn children in order to save them from a potentially difficult life or from burdening the national social system.

More simply, it is better to kill than to let live.

The question and its premise are filled with illogical assumptions and conundrums. Here are just a few:

- To assume it is better to be dead than alive is not a testable theory. Since most of us have not died and come back to life, there is little evidence to support that death is preferable to life. While many faiths hold that the unborn and infants are ushered into a positive afterlife, these faiths do not advocate intentionally causing death in order to find out if it is true.

- Ironically, we are horrified and saddened by suicide. When someone voluntarily elects death over life, assuming that death is better than life, we call it a tragedy. But when parents voluntarily take the life of their unborn child, assuming death is better than life, we call it a right and a choice.

- When children grow up in difficult circumstances, it can be sad and challenging. Whether it is a foster home, a poverty-stricken home, a fatherless home, or some other real challenge, the community should be a help and assistance to the child. But should we terminate a life in order to prevent the struggle? Can we not understand that struggles and challenges are part of being human and, in an abundance of cases, contribute to our health, growth, productivity, and success as humans?

  While there remain too many sad circumstances of young people from single-parent homes getting involved with drugs, alcohol, abuse, and violence, there is a multitude of examples of young people conquering those demons and rising to amazing levels of personal and professional success. President Barack Obama is just one example of a person raised in a single-parent home in less than desirable circumstances. He rose to the most powerful position in the world.

Is it really up to us to take a life before allowing her a chance to experience life in its fullness, with its joys and sorrows, triumphs and struggles, laughter and tears?

This premise is population control in disguise. It assumes that being poor, living in foster homes, or growing up in a disadvantaged community makes you less of a person. The life-affirming man sees wonderful potential, redemption, and value in each person, regardless of race, color, socio-economic status, or government program.

We also forget that living Americans are typically highly productive. Researcher Dennis Howard calculates that we have lost around $45 trillion in gross domestic product to abortion since 1973.[290] Why is Social Security failing? We've terminated the lives of people who were to help pay for it.

In addition, when society takes the role of determining which innocent person lives or dies, it takes a dangerous turn difficult to reverse. If society can determine the value of unborn life, it can determine the value of any other life.

4. "You just want to save babies. You do nothing to help those who are born." I hesitate to even include this point, but this perspective does seem to erode man's desire to protect life. It is a form of intimidation that abortion proponents use to silence others.

The idea is, if you are working to protect babies and women from abortion and not adopting, providing foster care, or mentoring someone, you are not really concerned about life. You are just concerned about babies. Your commitment to rescue the unborn is shallow, and you are ignoring the needs of those who are already born.

The argument is logically flawed on numerous levels:

- A life-affirming man acknowledges that rescuing a life from death is a primary and urgent goal. To say that goal should be subordinated to the care of a living person not in danger of death is problematic. Should we close all emergency rooms and just provide care for non-life-threatening injuries? Let's shut down fire departments and build safer houses.

Let's close down police departments and, instead, work on community centers.

Do we criticize ER doctors because they aren't general practitioners? Do we disdain firemen because they aren't building the homes they are protecting? Do we condemn policemen because they aren't teachers?

Of course not. Our society understands that protecting and preserving life is the preeminent goal. Providing care for the living is essential, but it does no good if we aren't saving lives from death in the first place.

- The argument assumes that life-affirming men aren't engaged in other important social work. The assumption is invalid. I know of scores of life-affirming people who are heavily involved in other work, including adoption, foster care, church programs, mentoring, youth groups, social services, welfare programs, and a host of other quality-of-life initiatives. Most life-affirming people are concerned for the unborn and for families to the extent they give generously of their time, energy, and resources to save lives and to improve lives at all stages.

- In any given society, people play a variety of roles. To say a life-affirming man doesn't care about society just because he works to rescue babies does not mean he isn't playing a vital part. We would say the same about someone involved in caring for a born person. We should all be grateful for people who are working to help those around them at any stage of life and, in fact, most of us are.

5. We shouldn't work to stop abortion. We should work to stop unplanned pregnancy. This is a common statement, even from those professing to be life affirming. They have an innate understanding that the primary causes of abortion are rooted in sexual promiscuity, pornography, the breakdown of marriage and family, and a host of other issues.

When given this statement, I'll generally reply, "So you would advocate shutting down all cancer treatment centers in order to fund more cancer research centers?"

"Or perhaps we should shut down all ERs in favor of accident prevention educational programs?"

The flaw in the statement is to assume that the abortion epidemic is a linear problem. If we stop the cause, we'll stop the effect.

First, abortion is not a linear problem. It is more of a matrix with a host of causes, effects, symptoms, conditions, and circumstances. Secondly, refusing to stop abortions in favor of only doing prevention work results in millions of deaths and family ruin. To ignore the deaths in favor of prevention is to devalue those lives along with abortion proponents. It is akin to converting ambulances into hearses.

This is not to say we shouldn't be working hard to identify and help stop the causes of abortion. But to do so at the expense of saving children, right now, today, is horribly unethical and egregious.

Additionally, in many cases, an unplanned pregnancy is the catalyst for a positive change in the life of the parents. Sometimes the boyfriend will be prompted to seek gainful employment to provide for his unexpected child. A mother may finally get off drugs because she now cares for someone else more than for herself. Grandparents enter the picture and find themselves renewed with the task of helping to care for a grandchild.

We tend to think of an unplanned pregnancy as universally negative. But, as all parents know, a baby changes everything. And those changes can very often be extremely positive for the entire family, even if the baby was not expected. A baby often brings out the best in us, teaches us self-sacrifice, and can be the catalyst to tremendous growth and life change for the parents and extended family.

At this point, you might be exasperated. Men are apparently complete pigs, unable to control their sexual urges. They have been so feminized as to be almost unrecognizable. Most men ignore abortion, and many are quiet supporters of it—both inside and outside the church. Those who support and affirm life are few and far between. And they are constantly tempted to give up their passion and commitment due to strong social forces, intimidation, and the inability to legally do anything about it. The culture firmly believes men are meaningless in the abortion decision, and most men have accepted that fate.

Really, is there anything men can do to truly promote gender equality, rescue unborn children, and save the American family from the abortion holocaust?

Yes.

We can end it.

CHAPTER 10

MEN CAN END IT

I grew up in a stable, caring home with parents who have now been married for over 45 years. I stayed away from trouble through high school and studied music in college. One night at a social event, I looked across the room and saw a beautiful woman. Jessica was captivating, and I was hooked. Six months later I asked her on a date. A few years later, I married her.

We started life together as a couple in Pittsburgh, Pennsylvania. I started working part time at a local radio station, and my wife worked as an elementary school teacher. We were active in our church, in our community, and had all the typical hopes and dreams of young, married couples.

A few years later, Jess became pregnant. We were excited and scared, like most new parents. The pregnancy had its ups and downs, but on October 28, 1999, our first son was born. I was 26 years old.

My upbringing, education, and young married life couldn't have been more normal. I grew up in church, followed the teachings and leading of Jesus Christ, and tried to be a good guy. Most people liked me, and I liked most people.

I was passionately supportive of life-affirming efforts if anyone asked me. I knew the Bible verses about life, and we donated to a local pregnancy resource center. I even gave them some free consulting.

But sitting in that delivery room in October of 1999, holding my own son, my firstborn, something changed. A new life was sitting in my arms. Helpless, innocent, and ... mine.

I remember contemplating the gravity of abortion at that moment, wondering how we, as a culture, could end so many helpless, innocent lives. My baby, my son, could have just as easily been aborted if my life had been different.

That day was the beginning of a new journey. I began to intentionally research and learn more about abortion and its impact on women, men, and society.

Eight years later, a good friend of mine asked if I wanted to do some groundbreaking work to rescue babies from abortion.

Two years after that, Online for Life was born. We now work to rescue families from abortion across America, using compassion, grace, and education as our tools. Online for Life employs quite a few men—all of whom have committed themselves to helping end abortion in America.

I tell you this story for one reason: to admit that I spent the majority of my life blissfully unaware of the harm, hurt, discrimination, and death that abortion demands. I knew abortion existed, but I did nothing—nothing—to help anyone. I was content to live in my safe, comfortable bubble, free from any responsibility to rescue babies and parents from abortion.

Over the last few years, I've had the honor of speaking with numerous post-abortive men and women. Their stories have further awakened me to the pain and tragedy of abortion. And I now realize that abortion's tentacles reach far beyond the baby in the womb. They stretch out to hurt parents, siblings, extended family, communities, states, and our nation.

Abortion is not an issue. It is THE issue.

So, men, what now? Are you like me? Going about your life, acknowledging that around one in three adults are post-abortive, that a child loses his or her life every 25 seconds, that abortion has wreaked havoc on virtually every aspect of American life? Did you assume abortion was just a woman's issue, instead of a plague that is destroying women's rights and gender equality?

If you've read this far and remain firmly in support of abortion, I want to thank you for taking the time to read a contrary book. Few people make the effort to read books that articulate opposing views. You and I are in disagreement, but I welcome your feedback and look forward to productive dialogue in the future. I am well aware that many, many people hold fast to the idea that abortion is a woman's right, is central to women's health, and elevates women in society. I hope I've given you some facts and perspectives to think about.

Perhaps you were uncertain about abortion's impact on women and society and this book has caused you to think more often and more critically about abortion. Keep questioning, keep learning, and keep digging. There is far too much at stake to walk away and do nothing.

And if you are in the category of men who have been awakened, emboldened, and convicted by the book, I urge you to read on. If you were already pursuing true gender equality by working to end abortion in America, allow me to say thank you. Let's move forward together.

As noted earlier, women will not be restored to true equality with men, and unborn lives will not be rescued from abortion for good until men, *en masse*, rise up to partner with women in the effort. This is not a sexist statement. It is reflective of the unified effort required to move a country from accepting abortion to being repulsed by it.

Is it possible? Of course it is. Men and women joined together in the 1800s to stem abortion in a movement that was effective for decades. Other dark times in history have been enlightened through men and women working together. William Wilberforce took a 5,000-year tradition of slavery and turned it on its head in one lifetime, and he engaged women and men in the quest to rid the vast British Empire of that grave social injustice.

Throughout history, great movements in social justice have come about when men and women partnered together.

So, men, here are the steps to rise from silence, join our sisters and brothers who are already gaining ground, and drive abortion from America's shores.

ALL MEN

Get off the damn porn. Stop sleeping with someone other than your wife. Stop moving from woman to woman, using them for your own selfish gratification and then tossing them away when you are done with them.

It's sleazy, disrespectful, self-centered, and you give our gender a bad reputation.

Plus, you are going to get someone killed. Like an innocent baby. Or two.

Porn

There is precious little research on the connection between pornography and abortion, mainly because there are very few research organizations willing to take on the topic. Plus, the vast majority of money is poured into abortion-favoring research groups.

Porn is a huge, extremely powerful industry.

So, while there is very little credible work being done on this connection, allow me to posit a theory.

Porn has been linked to sexual promiscuity for decades. It has been identified as a cause of extramarital affairs and multiple sex partners. A Marriage and Religion Research Institute report concludes, "[U]sers of pornography have a higher likelihood of contracting a sexually transmitted disease or fathering an out-of-wedlock pregnancy."[291]

It's obvious that promiscuity of any sort opens the door to a host of STIs, including HIV and AIDS. There are 20 million new STIs each year, and a total of 110 million infections among men and women in the U.S., according to the Centers for Disease Control. The cost to treat these infections is $16 billion annually.[292] And it's completely avoidable. For the unmarried, abstinence is the only form of truly "safe sex" known to man (or woman), and for married couples, faithfulness inside marriage will allay any and all concerns. "You have an extremely minimal chance of catching one of over 25 different sexually transmitted infections, many of which are incurable and can cause cancer," when you practice abstinence, as the Medical Institute for Sexual Health points out.[293]

And, I submit, sexual promiscuity also leads to unplanned pregnancies that are ending in abortion. It's not exactly rocket science to connect the dots here.

Your porn habit may result in the death of another human being. Is your porn that important to you?

Outside of the impending destruction of your marriage, other relationships, and your own character, there is the potential death of an unborn child.

Look, every red-blooded American man is tempted by porn, including yours truly. We are surrounded by it, saturated by it, and we can't get through an NFL game without being confronted with it.

And there are many guys who are full-on addicted to it. For them, it's not a habit—it's a necessity.

Gentlemen, there is nothing good that comes out of porn. Nothing. Do not pass "Go;" do not collect $200. Get all of the help, accountability, counseling, and intervention you need. You may end someone's life if you don't.

Stop Having an Affair

I have had the privilege of counseling men who have had affairs. Every one of them would tell you it was a horrible, terrible mistake. They would openly confess they traded cheap sex for a lasting, committed relationship. All it brought was pain.

Guys, an affair is an abortion risk, plain and simple. You cheat on your wife: you get the other woman pregnant. Now your secret has turned into living, breathing evidence of your indiscretion. The logical solution? Abort the child, and no one is ever the wiser.

Go work on your marriage. We tend to think all of the stuff that is wrong in our marriage is her fault. News flash: it is most likely our fault. Fix yourself, and your marriage will improve. You are probably the problem, anyhow.

Stop Sleeping Around

You unmarried guys who like to bed multiple women are a huge risk to unborn children—and an affront to the female gender. And you make the rest of us look bad. Not only are you unwilling to commit to a woman before you sleep with her, you don't have the decency to commit to her when you get her pregnant.

I know we live in a sex-saturated culture. I know we continue to treat traditional marriage like it is old fashioned and out of style. I know abstinence is treated like pure folly in the public schools and many other venues.

You are the men who love the power that abortion affords you. You are the men who drive the abortion industry, line the pockets of abortion providers, and are famous for saying, "It's your decision, honey. I'll support you in whatever you decide."

As much as I'd love to say kind and sensitive things to you, here's the truth. You are a boy who never grew up. You use women to satisfy the sexual urges you don't have the discipline and maturity to control. You talk about women's rights and equality because it gives you a pass on your lifestyle, and you are the first in line to defend abortion rights. And you only do that so that you can continue to sleep with whomever you want.

Grow up. Find a man who has been committed to his wife for 20 years, and be like that guy. Stop modeling yourself after the mindless pimps on TV and YouTube, and acknowledge you don't give a rip about women unless they give you what you want.

You are the face of abortion and the reason women in America continue to be exploited.

A NOTE TO WOMEN

Would you please stop entertaining and sleeping with these guys? If you are sleeping with a married guy, you are being used. If you are sleeping with a guy who hasn't married you, you are being used. "Living together" is just a fancy term for, "I want to use you for sex until I'm tired of you."

Please, kick him to the curb and go find a decent man who accepts you, treats you like an equal, and will give up his life for you. Anyone else is just a waste of time.

Besides, there is a good chance this loser is going to get you pregnant. Who is going to be left with the decision about what to do with the baby? You. Who is the only legally responsible party? You. Who will bear the brunt of the abortion? You.

You are worth more than that. You deserve to be treated better, respected more, and protected by someone who is willing to commit the rest of his life to you. Don't settle for anything less.

A MESSAGE TO POST-ABORTIVE MEN

Allow me to address those post-abortive men reading the book right now. I am convinced the power to end abortion rests with you. Your stories, your pain, and your perspective are what is missing from the abortion dialogue in America.

When was the last time we saw a news story about a post-abortive man? It's very rare.

Aerosmith's Steven Tyler has unveiled his pain at allowing his child to be aborted. Tyler was 25 in 1975, when he and his 14-year-old, live-in girlfriend decided to abort their child. "It was a big crisis," he recalled in *Walk This Way*, Aerosmith's tell-all memoir. "It's a major thing when you're growing something with a woman, but they convinced us that it would never work out and would ruin our lives."

Tyler's girlfriend, whom he later dropped, had a saline abortion, a heinous procedure in which a salt solution is used to slowly burn and kill the baby. Tyler witnessed it all. "You go to the doctor and they put the needle in her belly and they squeeze the stuff in and you watch. And it comes out dead. I was pretty devastated. In my mind, I'm going, 'Jesus, what have I done?'"[294]

After Michael Jackson's death, it was revealed he had written a song about an abortion loss, possibly his own. Recorded in the 1980s, "Song Groove (A/K/A Abortion Papers)" includes the narrator's protest of his partner's decision to abort their child:

Those abortion papers
Signed in your name against the words of God
Those abortion papers
Think about life, I'd like to have my child[295]

1. Start with your own heart, your own life.

These are powerful testimonies, and there are tens of thousands, perhaps millions of men who have the same story. Their stories need to be told, even if it is just to one person, one couple, one teenage kid who doesn't know the first thing about it.

Your story, though painful, is also redemptive.

If you have not yet come to grips with your own post-abortive past, healing must occur first.

Charlie is a man in his seventies. He took his girlfriend to get an abortion in 1972. Shortly afterward, he straightened out his life and got married to another woman, to whom he has been wed for almost 40 years. They have children and grandchildren. Still, he was never able to escape the pain and guilt he felt from that abortion, which he even kept a secret from his wife. He ultimately found healing after he attended a Rachel's Vineyard retreat for post-abortive men and women.

After the retreat, he wanted to jump into some kind of life-affirming activity. So when his church encouraged his participation in 40 Days for Life, a 40-day period of prayer and fasting to end abortion, he got involved.

> He eagerly went straight to the front lines [outside an abortion facility] to pray and talk with the younger men taking women in to have abortions, sharing with them the mistake he still regretted nearly forty years later. He smiled broadly. "And now, standing here praying and sharing my story with these younger men, God is healing me. I have never felt such peace—and such joy."[296]

How can you escape the bonds of your part in abortion?

Recognize your role, take responsibility, and find healing. You may very well not have known that you were actively or passively ending a life.

The mother of your child may have insisted on getting the abortion. You may have been getting pressure from family members, friends, or other authority figures to abort.

Still, you were involved and need to own up to it.

Recognizing and taking responsibility for your active or passive role in an abortion is imperative if you want to join the effort to save others.

Forgiveness, peace, and joy are all on the table for you. But taking ownership and confessing your role are necessary steps.

This is not a book about post-abortive counseling, and I am the furthest thing from a counselor. I have listed some excellent resources at the end of the book if this is a need in your life. I encourage you to immediately move towards the path to healing and recovery. Your family and relationships may depend on it. And, when you experience forgiveness and peace, you may be ready to help others avoid your struggles.

As a follower of Christ, I am absolutely certain you can find forgiveness and redemption in Him. I encourage you to seek Him out.

2. Share your story with trusted loved ones.

I'm asking you to do something that is extremely difficult. In some cases, my request may not be appropriate.

However, you may be realizing that the time has come to end your silence. There may be a family member contemplating abortion who doesn't know you were responsible for one. You may have a teenage son or daughter who believes abortion is a reasonable solution, and they have no idea the pain and tragedy you have suffered.

Your own relationships may be suffering, and you haven't been able to identify why until now. There may be strain, distance, and anger for reasons that are now known.

I don't make this request lightly, and I urge you to carefully consider the cost of sharing your story. You might consider seeking the counsel of a trusted friend, a priest, a pastor, or a counselor before you tell a family member. You could very well risk harming relationships, being ashamed, and creating tension between you and others if you share your past.

Your story could also mean the difference between life and death for an unborn child. And your story will very likely save the life of a child not yet conceived. Your story may be enough to convince a family member who currently sees abortion as a solution that it is, in fact, terribly damaging to all involved. Your life-ending decision years ago could save a life in the future.

3. Speak your testimony publicly.
Share your story with a broader audience.

This takes a lot of guts, guys. There isn't a man alive who, having come to grips with his abortive past, wants to tell strangers about it. And this isn't an appropriate step for all men.

But it is for many of you. And we won't end abortion in America until those of you who can, do.

Why? Because those forces and organizations who actively promote abortion fear you most. Your courage to take responsibility for the abortion, to admit you used and exploited a woman, and to admit your mistakes, is the most powerful tool in the effort to end abortion.

The reason is this: It takes a strong man to admit he has wronged someone. It takes a strong man to share that publicly. We need strong men.

And your story is not only about failure and harm; it is about redemption and moving forward. It is about using your mistakes and selfishness and turning them into triumphs and selflessness.

When America learns that thousands, tens of thousands, even hundreds of thousands of men are willing to admit their abortions were wrong, that they harmed women, children, and families, America will begin to wake up and realize we've made an awful, horrendous mistake.

And we will work together to rectify that mistake.

You may be shamed; you may be judged. You may lose friends or family members. I certainly hope that isn't the case. But I promise you you'll also have advocates, supporters, and companions. And you can count me among them.

There is a safe, non-political, non-partisan site for men and women who wish to share their post-abortion stories. Whether or not you choose to remain anonymous, I invite you to share your story at www. abortionmemorial.com. This site is intended to be an appropriate, honoring place for post-abortive parents who want to heal.

ALL MEN WHO WANT TO END ABORTION

We won't end abortion in America until men individually choose to live their lives in a manner that rejects selfishness. Abortion exists because of male selfishness. And it will continue to exist as long as men continue to seek their own power, control, and pleasure.

Let's review the two primary social reasons abortion was promoted by men: population control and eugenics.

Population control is, as evidenced by its name, about control. It's about power. It's about one group having the authority to control another. One group decides a population needs to be curbed or eliminated altogether because they believe they are smarter and wiser than the other group.

The rationale may be trumped up with well-intended sentiments. The group in control may be trying to ensure that the world has enough food, that poverty is eliminated, or that education thrives. All of those are worthwhile endeavors.

But all of those may be addressed without aborting humans or sterilizing women.

The issue of starving people in the world is not about the abundance of food. The world produces more than enough food for every person on the planet.[297] Poverty is a drastic and real problem in many nations. But is the primary issue the size of the population or other pivotal factors such as corruption, economic climate, social discrimination, or form of government?

The same logic applies to the uneducated and illiterate. Is it the size and reproductive rate of the populace that is to blame for the state of education, or are the primary causes related to culture, form of government, and the disposition of people in power?

There is a vast difference between educating a family and forcing a populace to practice population control. There is a vast difference between an individual family choosing to use non-abortive means to determine the size of their family and a group in power dictating the size of their family.

The first is an attempt to empower; the second is an attempt to overpower.

Eugenics has the guts to admit it is population control for only certain races or people groups. It takes the position that one race should have the right to determine the growth of another.

This is also disguised in socially acceptable language. Eugenics promotes the control over another race for its own good. They may be poor, uneducated, and unruly. So the solution is to sterilize them, force them to use birth control, or make abortion a vital part of the culture, so they eliminate themselves.

There are awful assumptions embedded in these two philosophies. The primary one is that adding new members of the population increases the problems of that population. Yet, often population growth can actually help solve the problems ailing a nation and help it flourish. Would anyone doubt that America has grown more technologically and medically advanced—and stronger as a nation—as its population has increased?

This doesn't mean growth doesn't have challenges. But America is the wealthiest, most prosperous nation on the planet. Should we have purposefully stayed at 50 million people to limit the growth? Should an outside nation or group have a say over our own reproductive rights?

Both population control and eugenics are elitist philosophies. And they are both primarily about power—attempting to solve real needs of other people groups by addressing population growth and ignoring other primary factors that cause social challenges.

Population control and eugenics are large-scale manifestations of man's arrogance and selfishness.

The personal reason for men pushing abortion is sexual liberation. Men in America enjoy complete freedom to sleep with whomever they choose without legal, social, or cultural responsibility for the outcome of their actions related to a pregnancy.

It is the height of selfishness. Men feel they have the right to express the deepest of intimacies with women with no sign of commitment or support for said women. And our culture has devolved to the point where many women think this is just how it is.

And, when a woman has an unplanned pregnancy, the man can walk away from the situation without any responsibility.

Unplanned pregnancy is obviously an enormous factor contributing to abortions. Unplanned pregnancies are most often caused by selfish men. The solution? Stop being selfish, and then watch unplanned pregnancies decline and abortion go away.

Whether or not men are motivated by social and global reasons (population control and eugenics), or personal reasons (sexual freedom), abortion is about men exercising power and control over women, either nationally or personally.

Consequently, men must take up the mantle of service, sacrifice, and selflessness if we are to achieve true gender equality and rescue unborn children from death in the womb.

We end abortion by being respectful, moral men who see women as true equals of infinite value.

We end abortion by confronting social challenges through means other than dictating reproduction rights.

We end abortion by making a personal, committed decision to stop using women for our own sexual pleasure.

MEN ENDING ABORTION ON A NATIONAL SCALE

On a larger scale, there are a number of ways men can rise up and work to end abortion in America.

1. Mentor other men. Researcher Catherine Coyle in her study, "Men and Abortion: Finding Healing, Restoring Hope," says:

Mature male mentors are needed to teach younger men about the importance of chastity, commitment in relationships, and responsible parenting. Mentors can serve as role models as they demonstrate the behaviors that foster spiritual and psychological health in marital, paternal and fraternal relationships.[298]

Your willingness to teach, train, and share your life with other men is an essential piece of the abortion puzzle. This may or may not involve a commitment to an organization like Big Brothers/Big Sisters, a local youth group, a community organization, or a social service agency. Just working with your own sons, the neighborhood kids, or young men in your church can be a huge influence.

Whether formal or informal, be a truthful role model to other men in your community. Talk about abortion, sex, marriage, pornography, and how to properly treat a woman. Keep in mind that many people are more influenced by what is caught than what is taught. In other words, live out what you say.

2. Carefully research the use of birth control. The purpose of this book is not to discuss the moral implications of using birth control within a family. However, if you have made the decision to use birth control as a means of dictating the size of your family, do your homework.

Life begins at conception, not at implantation. If you are using a method of birth control that negatively impacts implantation, you could unknowingly be using an abortifacient substance.

Keep in mind some birth control products state that life begins at implantation, not conception. While many in the medical community, and some pharmaceutical companies, claim that these drugs do not cause abortions, they may not properly understand the facts of life.

For more information on this very important topic, I refer you to a short brochure by Randy Alcorn called, "Does the Birth Control Pill Cause Abortions?" It is free and widely available online.

3. Become involved and help grow life-affirming organizations in your area. When Planned Parenthood opened a surgical abortion clinic in his hometown of College Station, Texas, David Bereit reluctantly got involved, at his wife's prodding, to oppose it. He agreed to serve on the board of the Coalition for Life, the group launched in opposition to the new Planned Parenthood facility, and wound up the chairman after his first meeting. The chairman had resigned just before the meeting and, as David put it, he "didn't say, 'No,' fast enough." Despite his own sense of inadequacy, he saw the need and felt called to serve:

> I had no grand vision, no compelling drive to lead this mission. But I couldn't shake the inner conviction that had begun on that sidewalk. In my mind's eye I kept seeing the faces of the women I'd seen entering the abortion facility and their downcast eyes as they left. Everything about the place felt so wrong, and I had an inner sense that God wanted me to try to right that wrong.[299]

His initial efforts at the Coalition didn't prove fruitful, so he decided to resign his post at the end of his three-year term. But at the fundraising banquet at which his resignation was announced, the speaker, life-affirming leader Joe Scheidler, encouraged the audience to overcome their fears and do what is right even if they had no desire to do so. "There's somebody in this room who is supposed to do this work full time," Scheidler said, "somebody who is supposed to take a leadership role in this work." That caught David's attention, and he left the gathering, he writes, "with a new stirring in my heart. Maybe I did have a role."

Soon after, he and his wife came to the conclusion that he would begin seeking to end abortion, full-time, in College Station, Texas.

> I went home and talked to Margaret. We talked to our pastor. We prayed fervently. As much as we knew we were giving up—the company car, the salary, the health benefits, all the bonuses, and fancy dinners out with the doctors—all we had to do was weigh that against the innocent children's lives and mothers' well-being at stake, and even though we were terrified, we knew this was God's call.[300]

Now Bereit helps lead 40 Days for Life, the largest life-affirming mobilization in history, an effort that has helped save more than 7,000 unborn children from abortion since 2007. To date, more than a half million people have participated in 40 Days for Life campaigns in 501 cities and 19 countries. More than 40 abortion clinics have closed, and 83 abortion clinic workers have quit as a result of 40 Days for Life campaigns.

There are a host of life-affirming organizations across the country. Some are involved politically, some judicially. Some are involved with the public, providing compassion, truth, care, and connections to other local services.

Most of these are called pregnancy resource centers, crisis pregnancy centers, or pregnancy care centers. They are typically local non-profits who work with the abortion-minded people in their areas.

The vast majority of these centers are staffed by women; they are desperate for men as volunteers and staff. Often times they have abortion-minded men coming in, and they have no mentors to talk to them.

Want to save lives and help end abortion? Get to know your local pregnancy center and get involved.

A list of great organizations working to save women, men, and babies from abortion is included in the Resources section at the back of this book.

4. Use your specific gifts and talents. Laws follow culture. *Roe v. Wade* was handed down in 1973 because some very determined Americans wanted abortion to be legal. Abortion will stay legal until enough life-affirming women and men act, and the culture no longer wants it so.

We are now many decades into the abortion culture in America, and our society continues to approach abortion from opposing views.

Women will continue to be harmed and used, men will continue to suffer, and babies will continue to be lost until the social tide turns against abortion.

How do we regain a society that respects women and life?

We need look no further than social reformer William Wilberforce to find the answer.

His approach to ending slavery in England (and the West Indies) was remarkably comprehensive, taking advantage of most of the media of his day, various realms of influence, and numerous approaches to educating the public.

Political: Wilberforce used his power and influence in Parliament to keep the slavery issue in front of his fellow politicians for years. He continually submitted legislation to end the slave trade, though in the early years there was no chance of its passage. He was relentless in repeating his message. And, near the end of his life, his hard work in government paid off.

Media: Wilberforce printed bulletins, held live events (including bringing people on board slave ships to smell the stench of death and see the bloodstains), gave speeches, wrote letters, and used every educational tool available. And, with persistence, it worked. By the time slavery was made illegal in England, the culture found it repulsive. His committed approach to educating his nation worked.

Community Organization: Wilberforce started a very large number of associations and movements during his lifetime. Not all were specific to slavery, but all were dedicated to the betterment of society in general. Some were dedicated to the ethical treatment of animals, many were centered on promoting common decency, and others were specific to the slave trade.

Wilberforce was masterful at engaging people from all walks of life to be a part of something far bigger than himself.

I commend Eric Metaxas' stellar biography of Wilberforce to you, *Amazing Grace*. Not only does it provide a wonderful insight into Wilberforce as a man, it provides an effective blueprint of how to mobilize people to engage a cultural issue in order to right a wrong, restore culture so that it is edifying to all, and protect people of all races, nations, genders, and stages of development.

You come hard-wired with useful gifts and talents. Determine how your specific gifts can work to end abortion. Then go do it.

5. Lead. While the media, pop culture, aggressive pro-abortion factions, and extreme feminists continue to attempt to feminize the American male, will you allow those efforts to be successful?

Men, we are built to lead. We fall down; we fail. We've screwed some things up. But we are wired to bounce back, admit our errors, and lead.

This new generation of life-affirming leaders will be different.

We won't lead in order to grab power. We will lead to serve.

We won't lead so that other populations are diminished, controlled, or eliminated. We will lead so that these populations flourish economically, socially, spiritually, and culturally.

We won't treat certain people groups as less equal or valuable than others. Each race, nation, and group has unique, infinite value. Each group is special and is to be protected.

We won't discriminate based on race. We reject eugenics, population control, sterilization, abortion, and all other efforts to diminish minority groups. And we welcome our brothers and sisters from all races to our movement to end abortion in America.

We won't discriminate based on handicap. We find abortion based on birth defect, disease, or genetic abnormality reprehensible. All life is infinitely valuable, even if that life does not match society's definition of value.

We will no longer exploit women for our social or personal gain. We recognize women are equal to men and both have infinite value. We will work for true gender equality, recognizing and educating our nation that abortion, though legal, is inherently immoral and discriminatory. It is undeniably harmful to individual women and the female gender, as a whole. It widens the gender gap, essentially lowering women to a tool for misguided social agendas or personal pleasure.

We recognize that abortion is rampant in America because of unplanned pregnancy. Thus we will, as individual men and as a gender, stop engaging in behaviors and actions that cause unplanned pregnancies. We reject pornography, recognizing its direct connection to unwanted pregnancy. We will commit to sexual fidelity with our wives, not only for the benefit of our spouses, but for our families, our communities, and our country. We reject the sexual revolution and its resulting behaviors. We commit to the highest level of sexual integrity and will work aggressively to educate other men to the same.

We commit to a continuum of care for those families facing unplanned pregnancies. Rescuing a baby and family from abortion is not the last step; it is the first. We will work in our communities to identify, establish, promote, and build those services essential for the care of families facing a birth they did not originally anticipate. This includes adoption services for those courageous families who carry a child to term and place the baby into another family.

We will not judge, scorn, or deride our post-abortive brothers and sisters. There are too many victims, both born and unborn, to start casting stones. Instead, we welcome those post-abortive parents with open arms, commit to helping them heal, and give them an opportunity to rescue another family from their pain and suffering.

We will celebrate, affirm, and protect life at every stage, from conception to natural death.

We reject abortion in totality. There is no rational, moral reason for abortion in America or around the world. Unborn children are the weakest among us, with no voice of their own. They are innocent, having committed no offense against us. They deserve every opportunity to live—not die.

We, as men, recognize and repent of our role in the promotion, legalization, and continuation of abortion in America. We acknowledge it is not hyperbole to say that the very fabric of American life depends on us.

We will, with humility, faithfulness, and relentless perseverance, commit our time, resources, energy, heart, and testimony to ending abortion in America.

And we will.

If you agree to lead, men, join us by signing the Life Pledge at www.thelifepledge.com.

RESOURCES

This list is by no means exhaustive, and I invite you to look for life-affirming local or national groups that resonate with you.

Share your post-abortive stories and honor aborted children:
AbortionMemorial.com

Sign the Life Pledge:
TheLifePledge.com

More information about this book:
AbortionExploitsWomen.com

For more information about Online for Life:
OnlineForLife.org
Facebook.com/OnlineforLife

Get involved with your local Pregnancy Resource Centers:
Care-Net.org
HeartbeatInternational.org

Or search online for the closest center in your area

Find help if you are a post-abortive man or woman:

MenandAbortion.net

FatherhoodForever.org

HopeAfterAbortion.com (Project Rachel)

Support other life-affirming organizations and efforts:

AUL.org

NRLC.org

40DaysForLife.com

MarchForLife.org

HeroicMedia.org

VitaeFoundation.org

180Movie.com

Support organizations doing life-affirming legal work:

LawofLifeProject.org

ACLJ.org

ADF.org

NIFLA.org

ThomasMore.org

ENDNOTES

1   *Roe v. Wade*, 410 U.S. 113. http://www.law.cornell.edu/supct/
     html/historics/USSC_CR_0410_0113_ZO.html

2   *Planned Parenthood of Southeastern Pa. v. Casey* (91-744), 505 U.S.
     833 (1992).

3   *Roe v. Wade*, 410 U.S.

4   "Unmarried Childbearing," FastStats, Centers for Disease Control.
     http://www.cdc.gov/nchs/fastats/unmarry.htm

5   Mark Mather, "U.S. Children in Single Mother Families,"
     Population Reference Bureau, May 2010.

6   Lawrence B. Finer, Lori F. Frohwirth, Lindsay A. Dauphinee,
     Susheela Singh and Ann M. Moore, "Reasons U.S. Women Have
     Abortions: Quantitative and Qualitative Perspectives," *Perspectives
     on Sexual and Reproductive Health*, 2005, 37(3), 113. https://www.
     guttmacher.org/pubs/journals/3711005.pdf

7   Kathleen McDonnell, *Not An Easy Choice: Re-Examining Abortion*
     (Toronto: Second Story Press, 2003) 59.

8   Connie Schultz, "Sorry, boys, but abortion is a women's issue,"
     Cleveland Plain Dealer, January 21, 2008. http://blog.cleveland.
     com/pdworld/2008/01/sorry_boys_but_abortion_is_a_w.html

9   Cynthia Gorney, *Articles of Faith: A Frontline History of the Abortion Wars* (New York: Simon and Schuster, 2000), 401.

10   Bernard Nathanson, with Richard N. Ostling, *Aborting America* (Garden City, New York: Doubleday, 1979), 171.

11   Gorney, *Articles of Faith*, 401.

12   Heart disease kills, according to the Centers for Disease Control but abortion takes the lives each year of about 1.2 million children annually. See "Fastats: Leading Causes of Death," Centers for Disease Control, http://www.cdc.gov/nchs/fastats/lcod.htm, and "U.S. Abortion Statistics," Abort73.com. http://www.abort73.com/abortion_facts/us_abortion_statistics/

13   "Facts on Induced Abortion in the United States," Guttmacher Institute, August 2011. http://www.guttmacher.org/pubs/fb_induced_abortion.html#4a

14   "Abortion for Profit," Abort73.com, September 3, 2010. http://www.abort73.com/abortion/abortion_for_profit/

15   Mark Crutcher, "Baby Body Parts for Sale," LifeDynamics.com, February 2000, updated March 2007. http://www.lifedynamics.com/abortion_information/baby_body_parts/

16   Barack Obama, "Statement by the President on *Roe v. Wade* Anniversary," Whitehouse.gov. http://www.whitehouse.gov/the-press-office/2012/01/22/statement-president-roe-v-wade-anniversary

17   "Hillary Clinton on Abortion," OntheIssues.org. http://www.ontheissues.org/senate/hillary_clinton_abortion.htm

18   http://en.wikipedia.org/wiki/Michael_Bloomberg#cite_ref-99

19   Ibid.

20   Ibid.

21   "A Message from Gwyneth Paltrow and Blythe Danner," http://operationrescue.org/images/dannerpaltrow%20email.pdf

22   http://www.nbcuniversalarchives.com/nbcuni/clip/5112663017_004.do

23   "Sex-Selection Abortion," House Report 112-496 - PRENATAL NONDISCRIMINATION ACT (PRENDA) OF 2012, http://

thomas.loc.gov/cgi-bin/cpquery/?&sid=cp112SUHud&r_n=hr496
.112&dbname=cp112&&sel=TOC_25644&

24   Abrevaya, Jason. 2009. "Are There Missing Girls in the United
     States? Evidence from Birth Data." *American Economic Journal:
     Applied Economics*, 1(2): 1-34. http://www.aeaweb.org/articles.
     php?doi=10.1257/app.1.2.1

25   "Roe v. Wade at 40: Most Oppose Overturning Abortion
     Decision," The Pew Forum on Religion and Public Life, January
     16, 2013. http://www.pewforum.org/Abortion/roe-v-wade-at-40.
     aspx

26   Scott Klusendorf, *The Case for Life: Equipping Christians to Engage
     the Culture* (Wheaton, Ill.: Crossway Books, 2009) 182-3.

27   Dr. Keith Ablow, "Men Should Be Allowed to Veto Abortions,"
     Foxnews.com, July 22, 2011. http://www.foxnews.com/
     opinion/2011/07/22/men-should-be-allowed-to-veto-
     abortions/#ixzz2IeIii0fe

28   David Bereit and Shawn Carney, *40 Days for Life* (Nashville:
     Capella Books, 2013) 106-8.

29   Phil McCombs, "Remembering Thomas," *Washington Post*,
     February 3, 1995. Posted at http://www.priestsforlife.org/
     postabortionrememberingthomas.htm

30   *Scott v. Sanford*, 60 U.S. (19 How.) 393 (1857).

31   *Roe v. Wade*, 410 U.S. 113 (1973). http://www.law.cornell.edu/
     supct/html/historics/USSC_CR_0410_0113_ZS.html

32   Ibid.

33   Ibid.

34   Ibid.

35   Keith Moore and T. V. N. Persaud, *The Developing Human:
     Clinically Oriented Embryology* (Philadelphia: Saunders/Elsevier,
     2008) 15 (emphasis added). Cited in Scott Klusendorf, *The Case
     for Life* (Wheaton, Illinois: Crossway Books, 2009) 35.

36   Text of an E-Mail from Sen. John Kerry (D-Ma.) on the Unborn
     Victims of Violence Act, June 27, 2003. http://www.nrlc.org/
     Unborn_Victims/kerryemailUVVA.html

37 From *Lysistrata*, quoted in Alvin J. Schmidt, *How Christianity Changed the World* (Grand Rapids, Michigan: Zondervan, 2001, 2004) 98.

38 Schmidt, *How Christianity Changed the World*, 97-101.

39 David H. Cherry, editor, *The Roman World: A Sourcebook* (Malden, Mass.: Blackwell Publishers, 2001) 51.

40 Philip Schaff, *The Person of Christ: The Miracle of History* (Boston: American Tract Society, 1865) 210. Cited in Alvin J. Schmidt, *How Christianity Changed the World* (Grand Rapids, Michigan: Zondervan, 2001, 2004) 101.

41 Talmud, Sotah, 19a, Cited in Gary R. Habermas and Michael L. Licona, *The Case for the Resurrection of Jesus* (Grand Rapids, Michigan: Kregel Publications, 2004) 72.

42 Gary R. Habermas and Michael L. Licona, *The Case for the Resurrection of Jesus* (Grand Rapids, Michigan: Kregel Publications, 2004) 72.

43 Sakuntala Narasimhan, *Sati: Widow Burning in India* (New York: Anchor Books, 1990) 27.

44 Dorothy K. Stein, "Women to Burn: Suttee as a Normative Institution," *Signs: Journal of Women Culture and Society* (Winter 1978) 253. Cited in Schmidt, *How Christianity Changed the World*, 116.

45 Schmidt, *How Christianity Changed the World*, 118-9.

46 Tocqueville, Alexis de, *Democracy in America* (London: Saunders and Otley, 1840) 106.

47 Modern History Sourcebook: The Declaration of Sentiments, Seneca Falls Conference, 1848. http://www.fordham.edu/halsall/mod/senecafalls.asp

48 Nonie Darwish, *Cruel and Usual Punishment* (Nashville: Thomas Nelson, 2008) 64.

49 Ibid., ix.

50 Farid Ahmed and Moni Basu, "Only 14, Bangladeshi girl charged with adultery was lashed to death," CNN.com, March 29, 2011.

http://edition.cnn.com/2011/WORLD/asiapcf/03/29/bangladesh.
lashing.death/index.html

51 Sabina Amidi, "I wed Iranian girls before execution," *The Jerusalem
Post*, July 19, 2009. http://www.jpost.com/IranianThreat/News/
Article.aspx?id=149091

52 "Rifqa Bary Granted U.S. Residency," 10TV.com, Tuesday
September 7, 2010. http://www.10tv.com/content/
stories/2010/09/07/story-columbus-rifqa-bary-us-citizen-granted.
html

53 Julia Dahl, ""Honor killing" under growing scrutiny in the U.S.,"
CBSNews.com, April 4, 2012. http://www.cbsnews.com/8301-
504083_162-57409395-504083/honor-killing-under-growing-
scrutiny-in-the-u.s/

54 Crime in the United States 2011, Forcible Rape, Federal Bureau of
Investigation. http://www.fbi.gov/about-us/cjis/ucr/crime-in-the-
u.s/2011/crime-in-the-u.s.-2011/violent-crime/forcible-rape

55 National Intimate Partner and Sexual Violence Survey Fact Sheet.
http://www.cdc.gov/ViolencePrevention/pdf/NISVS_FactSheet-a.
pdf

56 "Domestic Violence Facts," The National Coalition Against
Domestic Violence. http://www.ncadv.org/files/DomesticViolence
FactSheet%28National%29.pdf

57 Bureau of Justice Statistics Crime Data Brief, Intimate Partner
Violence, 1993-2001, February 2003. Cited in "Domestic
Violence Facts," The National Coalition Against Domestic
Violence. http://www.ncadv.org/files/DomesticViolenceFactSheet
%28National%29.pdf

58 Pamela Paul, "From Pornography to Porno to Porn: How Porn
Became the Norm," in *The Social Costs of Pornography: A Collection
of Papers* (Princeton, N.J.: Witherspoon Institute, 2010).

59 Mary Eberstadt, Mary Anne Layden, "The Social Costs of
Pornography: A Statement of Findings and Recommendations,"
The Witherspoon Institute and the Social Trends Institute, 2010,
p. 35.

60   Ibid., 25.

61   John D. Foubert, Matt W. Brosi, and R Sean Bannon.
      "Pornography viewing among fraternity men: Effects on bystander
      intervention, rape myth acceptance and behavioral intent to
      commit sexual assault." *Journal of Sex Addiction and Compulsivity*
      18 (2011): 212-31. Available at: http://works.bepress.com/john_
      foubert/7

62   "Fatal Addiction: Ted Bundy's Final Interview," PureIntimacy.org,
      http://www.pureintimacy.org/piArticles/A000000433.cfm

63   Edwin M. Hale, *The Great Crime of the Nineteenth Century*
      (Chicago: C.S. Halsey, 1867). Available at http://archive.org/
      stream/greatcrimeofnine00hale/greatcrimeofnine00hale_djvu.txt

64   Marvin Olasky, *Abortion Rites: A Social History of Abortion in
      America* (Wheaton, Illinois: Crossway Books, 1992), 291.

65   A. K., Gardner, "Physical Decline of American Women," *Health
      Reformer*, September 1876. In *Good Health*, Vol. 11, (Good Health
      Publishing Company, 1876) 259.

66   Olasky, *Abortion Rites*, 22.

67   Ibid., 102.

68   Serrin Foster, "How Men Convinced Women to be Pro-Abortion,"
      CatholicCulture.org, http://www.catholicculture.org/culture/
      library/view.cfm?recnum=111

69   Elizabeth Cady Stanton. *The Revolution*, February 5 and March 12,
      1868.

70   Mary Ann Glendon, "The Women of *Roe v. Wade,*" *First Things*,
      June/July 2003. http://www.firstthings.com/article/2007/01/the-
      women-of-roe-v-wade-34

71   Susan B. Anthony. *The Revolution*, July 8, 1869. Emphasis added.

72   "Alice Paul" entry in New World Encyclopedia. http://www.
      newworldencyclopedia.org/entry/Alice_Paul

73   Ibid.

74   Kate O'Beirne, "Pro-Life Women Fight For Feminism,"
      NationalReview.com, January 23, 2006. http://www.

nationalreview.com/articles/216565/pro-life-women-fight-feminism/kate-obeirne

75 *McDowall's Journal*, May 1833, p. 36. Quoted in Olasky, 141.

76 Ibid., April 1834, 31. Quoted in Olasky, 142.

77 *National Police Gazette*, February 14, 1846, 205. Quoted in Olasky, 149.

78 "The Evil of the Age," *New York Times*, August 23, 1871. Cited in Olasky, 153.

79 AMA Report on Criminal Abortion, 1859, http://www.abortionessay.com files/1859ama.html

80 Frederick N. Dyer, "How Abortion Became Illegal in the United States," Patheos.com, May 25, 2011. http://www.patheos.com/Resources/Additional-Resources/How-Abortion-Became-Illegal-in-the-United-States-Frederick-Dyer-05-25-2011.html

81 H.R. Storer, "Criminal Abortion: Its Prevalence, Its Prevention, and Its Relation to the Medical Examiner...," Microfiche #AN 0320 in the Adelaide Nutting Historical Nursing Microfilm Collection which is a microfiche of an offprint of the article in *Atlantic Medical Weekly* 1897, 209-218. Offprint page numbers 1-34, p. 12-13. Cited by Frederick Dyer in "John Preston Leonard's 'Quackery and Abortion:' Blueprint for Horatio Robinson Storer's Crusade Against Abortion?" http://horatiostorer.net/Quackery_and__Abortion.html#_ednref10

82 Joseph Meredith Toner, *Transactions of the American Medical Association*, Vol. 16 (Philadelphia: Collins Printer, 1866) 723.

83 Frederick N. Dyer, "How Abortion Became Illegal in the United States," Patheos.com, May 25, 2011. http://www.patheos.com/Resources/Additional-Resources/How-Abortion-Became-Illegal-in-the-United-States-Frederick-Dyer-05-25-2011.html

84 James Mohr, *Abortion in America* (New York: Oxford University Press, 1978) 240. Cited in Olasky, 198.

85 *Journal of the American Medical Association*, Vol. 46, (April 28, 1909) 1309. Cited in Olasky, 194.

86 Olasky, 194-6

87   Minutes of the Chicago Medical Society, Vol. 17, October 1905-
      June 1907. Cited in Olasky, 196.

88   Henry Marcy, "Education as a Factor in the Prevention of
      Criminal Abortion and Illegitimacy," *Journal of the American
      Medical Association*, Vol. 47 (1906, 1889). Cited in Olasky, 234-5.

89   Olasky, 235.

90   "Medicine: Abortions," *Time*, March 16, 1936. http://www.time.
      com/time/magazine/article/0,9171,755930,00.html

91   Dr. Frederick J. Taussig, *Abortion: Spontaneous and Induced:
      Medical and Social Aspects* (St. Louis: Mosby, 1936) 448. Cited in
      Olasky, 261.

92   Taussig, *Abortion*, 390. Cited in Samuel W. Calhoun, "Sowing the
      Wind, Reaping the Whirlwind: From Frederick Taussig's *Abortion:
      Spontaneous and Induced* (1936) to Warren Hern's *Abortion Practice*
      (1984)," http://uffl.org/vol10/calhoun10.pdf

93   *The Abortion Problem* (The Williams & Wilkins Co., 1944,
      publishing the proceedings of a 1942 conference), 28. Cited in
      Samuel W. Calhoun, "Sowing the Wind, Reaping the Whirlwind:
      From Frederick Taussig's *Abortion: Spontaneous and Induced* (1936)
      to Warren Hern's *Abortion Practice* (1984)." http://uffl.org/vol10/
      calhoun10.pdf

94   Mary Calderone, "Illegal Abortion as a Public Health Problem,"
      American Journal of Public Health, Vol. 50. No. 7. p. 949.
      http://www.ncbi.nlm.nih.gov/pmc/articles/PMC1373382/pdf/
      amjphnation00308-0022.pdf

95   *The Abortion Problem: Proceedings of the Conference Held Under
      the Auspices of the National Committee on Maternal Health, Inc.*
      (Baltimore: Williams and Wilkins, 1944) 50-2, 104. Cited in
      Olasky, 262.

96   Mary Calderone, ed., *Abortion in the United States* (New York:
      Hoeber-Harper, 1958) 166. Cited in Olasky, 263.

97   Calderone, ed., *Abortion in the United States*, 109. Cited in
      Olasky, 263.

98   Olasky, 273.

99   *Atlanta Constitution*, August 18, 1962, 30. Cited in Olasky, 280.

100   *The Gallup Poll, Public Opinion 1935-1971* (New York: Random House, 1972), 1984. Cited in Olasky, 281.

101   "The Cruel Abortion Law," *New York Times*, April 7, 1965.

102   Leslie J. Reagan, *When Abortion Was a Crime: Women, Medicine, and Law in the United States, 1867-1973* (Berkeley, Calif.: University of California Press, 1997) 222, see note 15 for list of states. Also see Sarah Kliff "CHARTS: How *Roe v. Wade* changed abortion rights," WashingtonPost.com, January 22, 2013. http://www.washingtonpost.com/blogs/wonkblog/wp/2013/01/22/charts-how-roe-v-wade-changed-abortion-rights/

103   Douglas Martin, "Lawrence Lader, Champion of Abortion Rights, Is Dead at 86," *New York Times*, May 10, 2006. http://www.nytimes.com/2006/05/10/nyregion/10lader.html?_r=1&

104   Bernard Nathanson, *The Hand of God* (Washington, D.C.: Regnery, 1996) 86.

105   Bernard Nathanson, with Richard N. Ostling, *Aborting America* (Garden City, New York: Doubleday, 1979) 31.

106   Elaine Woo, "Lawrence Lader, 86; Activist for Abortion Rights Whose Book Was Cited in *Roe* Case," *Los Angeles Times*, May 14, 2006. http://articles.latimes.com/2006/may/14/local/me-lader14

107   Margaret Sanger, *Woman and the New Race* (New York: Truth Publishing Co., 1920) 94. Quoted in Lawrence Lader, *Abortion II: Making the Revolution* (Boston: Beacon Press, 1974) 18.

108   Lawrence Lader, *Abortion II: Making the Revolution* (Boston: Beacon Press, 1974) ix.

109   Ibid.

110   David J. Garrow, *Liberty and Sexuality: The Right to Privacy and the Making of Roe v. Wade* (Berkeley, Calif.: University of California Press, 1994) 292.

111   Nathanson, with Ostling, *Aborting America*, 32.

112   Ibid., 32-33.

113   Ibid., 50.

114   Ibid., 53.

115   Ibid.

116   Bernard Nathanson, *The Hand of God* (Washington, D.C.: Regnery Gateway, 1996) 88.

117   Rosemary Oelrich Bottcher, "Men Launched the Movement to Legalize Abortion," FeministsforLife.org. http://feministsforlife. org/news/men-launched-the-movement-to-legalize-abortion.htm

118   Betty Friedan, *Life So Far: A Memoir* (New York: Simon & Schuster) 377.

119   Betty Friedan, *The Second Stage: With a New Introduction* (Cambridge, Mass.: Harvard Univ. Press, 1981, 1986 1991, 1998) 246–8, esp. 247.

120   Stella Morabito, "Feminist enablers of the war against women," *Washington Examiner*, March 11, 2012. http:// washingtonexaminer.com/feminist-enablers-of-the-war-against-women/article/361536#.UQQ6efL9V8M

121   Judith Blake, "Abortion and Public Opinion: The 1960-1970 Decade" 1971. Cited in Eva R. Rubin, editor, *The Abortion Controversy: A Documentary History* (Westport, Conn.: 1994) 107.

122   Edward Manier, William Thomas Liu, W. D. Solomon, *Abortion: New Direction for Policy Studies* (University of Notre Dame Press, 1977) 7.

123   Mary Meehan, "How Eugenics and Population Control Led to Abortion," MeehanReports.com. The article originally appeared under the title "The Road to Abortion" as a two-part series in *Human Life Review*, Fall 1998 & Winter 1999. See http://www. meehanreports.com/how-led.html

124   Adolf Meyer, editor, *Birth control: facts and responsibilities* (The Williams & Wilkins company, 1925) 48.

125   Margaret Sanger, *The Pivot of Civilization* (New York: Brentano's, 1922) (Kindle Location 866).

126   Ibid., Kindle Locations 284-6.

127   Lothrop Stoddard, *The Rising Tide of Color Against White World-Supremacy* (New York: Charles Scribner's Son, 1921) vi.

128 Madeline Gray, *Margaret Sanger: A Biography of the Champion of Birth Control* (New York, Richard Marek Publishers, 1979) 91.

129 Havelock Ellis, Spartacus Educational. http://www.spartacus. schoolnet.co.uk/TUhavelock.htm

130 George Grant, *Grand Illusions: The Legacy of Planned Parenthood* (Nashville: Cumberland House Publishing, 1988) 115.

131 Havelock Ellis, "The Sterilization of the Unfit," *Eugenics Review*, October 1909, 203-6. http://www.ncbi.nlm.nih.gov/pmc/articles/ PMC2986668/?page=1

132 Havelock Ellis, *The Task of Social Hygiene* (Boston and New York: Houghton Mifflin Company, 1913) 200.

133 Havelock Ellis, *The Problem of Race Regeneration* (London, New York: Cassell and Company, 1911) 69.

133 Ibid., 67.

134 Madeline Gray, *Margaret Sanger: A Biography of the Champion of Birth Control*, caption on unnumbered photo page.

135 Margaret Sanger, "Let's Talk It Over," 17 July 1939. The Public Writings and Speeches of Margaret Sanger. http://www. nyu.edu/projects/sanger/webedition/app/documents/show. php?sangerDoc=129007.xml

136 Ibid.

137 Ibid.

138 John Hunt, Ph.D., "Perfecting Humankind: A Comparison of Progressive and Nazi Views on Eugenics, Sterilization, and Abortion," *The Linacre Quarterly*, Vol. 66, February 199, No. 1, 30.

139 *The Woman Rebel*, Vol. 1, No. 1, March 1914. http://wyatt. elasticbeanstalk.com/mep/MS/xml/b3083963.html#b3083963

140 Margaret Sanger, *Family Limitation*, pamphlet, 1914, 5. http:// library.lifedynamics.com/Family%20Limitation/Family%20 Limitation.pdf

141 Madeline Gray, *Margaret Sanger*, 159, 280; Also see George Grant, *Grand Illusions: The Legacy of Planned Parenthood*

(Nashville: Cumberland House Publishing, 1988, 1992, 1998, 2000) 77.

142   Margaret Sanger, *An Autobiography* (New York: W. W. Norton, 1938) 185.

143   Ibid., 188.

144   Ibid., 217.

145   Robert Marshall, Charles Donovan, *Blessed are the Barren: The Social Policy of Planned Parenthood* (San Francisco: Ignatius Press, 1991) 280.

146   Ibid., 280.

147   Matthew James Connelly, *Fatal Misconception: The Struggle to Control World Population* (Cambridge, Mass.: Harvard University, 2008) 163.

148   Quoted in David J. Garrow, *Liberty and Sexuality: The Right to Privacy and the Making of Roe v. Wade* (Berkeley, Los Angeles: University of California Press, 1994, 1998) 271.

149   Alan Guttmacher, "The Genesis of Liberalized Abortion in New York: A Personal Insight," *Case Western Reserve Law Review*, vol. 23 (1972): 756-78. Quoted in Robert Marshall, Charles Donovan, *Blessed Are the Barren: The Social Policy of Planned Parenthood* (San Francisco: Ignatius Press, 1991), 258.

150   "Compulsory Population Control Foreseen," *Medical World News*, 6 June 6 1969, 11. Quoted in Robert Marshall, Charles Donovan, *Blessed Are the Barren: The Social Policy of Planned Parenthood* (San Francisco: Ignatius Press, 1991) 319.

151   William Stump, "Dr. Guttmacher - Still Optimistic About the Population Problem," *Baltimore Magazine* 63, no. 2 (Feb. 1970), 51-2. Quoted in Mary Meehan, "How Eugenics and Population Control Led to Abortion," MeehanReports.com. http://www.meehanreports.com/how-led.html

152   Frederick Osborn to P. R. U. Stratton, 12 Jan. 1966, AES Archives, folder on "Osborn, Frederick, Letters on Eugenics." Quoted in Mary Meehan, "How Eugenics and Population

Control Led to Abortion," MeehanReports.com. http://www.meehanreports.com/how-led.html

153 Mary Meehan, "How Eugenics and Population Control Led to Abortion," MeehanReports.com. http://www.meehanreports.com/how-led.html

154 Frederick Osborn, "Notes on Markle and Fox...," 25 Jan. 1974, Osborn Papers, folder on "Osborn - Paper - Notes on 'Paradigms or Public Relations...'" Quoted in Mary Meehan, "How Eugenics and Population Control Led to Abortion," MeehanReports.com. http://www.meehanreports.com/how-led.html

155 Paul Ehrlich, *The Population Bomb* (New York: Ballantine Books, 1968) 148.

156 Mary Meehan, "How Eugenics and Population Control Led to Abortion," MeehanReports.com. http://www.meehanreports.com/how-led.html

157 Francis Galton, "Eugenics: Its Definition, Scope and Aims," *Nature*, no. 1804, vol. 70 : 82, 26 May 1904. Galton.org. http://galton.org/cgi-bin/searchImages/search/essays/pages/galton-1905-socpapers-eugenics-definition-scope-aims_1.htm

158 Madison Grant, *The Passing of the Great Race: Or, The Racial Basis of European History* (New York: Charles Scribner's Sons, 1922) 60.

159 Gunnar Myrdal, *An American Dilemma: The Negro Problem and Modern Democracy*, Vol. 1 (New Brunswick, New Jersey: Transaction Publishers, 1996) 168.

160 Ibid., 170.

161 Ibid., 176.

162 Letter from Margaret Sanger to Dr. Clarence J. Gamble, 225 Adams St., Milton, Mass., December 10, 1939, Quoted in Robert Marshall, Charles Donovan, *Blessed are the Barren: The Social Policy of Planned Parenthood* (San Francisco: Ignatius Press, 1991) 18.

163 Gamble memo, undated but probably November or December 1939, Sanger Collection, Smith College, cited in Linda Gordon, *Women's Body, Women's Right: Birth Control in America* (New York: Penguin Books, 1990) 329. Also quoted in James Miller, "Betting

with lives: Clarence Gamble and the Pathfinder International," *PRI Review*, July/August 1996, Vol. 6, No. 4. http://www.pop.org/content/betting-with-lives-clarence-gamble-1752#endnote_anchor-21

164   Table 12, "Abortion Surveillance — United States, 2009 Surveillance Summaries," November 23, 2012. http://www.cdc.gov/mmwr/preview/mmwrhtml/ss6108a1.htm?s_cid=ss6108a1_w#Tab12

165   Susan Enouen, "Why Are Black Women Three Times More Likely to Have an Abortion?" LifeNews.com, 21 October 2012. http://www.lifenews.com/2012/10/21/why-are-black-women-three-times-more-likely-to-have-an-abortion/

166   Mark Crutcher, "Racial Targeting and Population Control," Life Dynamics Incorporated. http://lifenews.wpengine.netdna-cdn.com/wp-content/uploads/2011/08/LifeDynamicsRacialReport.pdf

167   Jeff Wise, "About That Overpopulation Problem," Slate.com, January 9, 2013. http://www.slate.com/articles/technology/future_tense/2013/01/world_population_may_actually_start_declining_not_exploding.html

168   Mary Meehan, "The 'Billionaire Brigade' of Population Controllers," MeehanReports.com. http://www.meehanreports.com/billionaire.html

169   "Secret billionaire club seeks population control," WorldNetDaily.com, June 24, 2009. http://www.wnd.com/2009/05/99105/#mkfemP5JG7MuqYbb.99

170   Bethany Monk, "Friday 5, Jonathan V. Last," Citizenlink.com, February 22, 2013. http://www.citizenlink.com/2013/02/22/friday-5-jonathan-v-last/

171   Table of Abuses and Violations by Country," Population Research Institute. http://www.pop.org/content/table-abuses-country

172   "*Post* documents Indian horror," Population Research Institute, *PRI Review*, September/October 1997. http://www.pop.org/content/post-documents-indian-horror-1597

173 Molly Moore, "Teeming India Engulfed by Soaring Birthrate; Sterilization Quotas Blasted As Inhuman and Coercive," *Washington Post*, August 21, 1994.

174 Carol Kuruvilla, "Horror in a mass sterilization camp: Unconscious Indian women were dumped in a field after undergoing a painful sterilization operation," *New York Daily News*, Thursday, February 7, 2013. http://www.nydailynews. com/news/national/indian-women-dumped-field-sterilization-operation-article-1.1258314

175 Rafael Romo, "Peruvian authorities reopen investigation into forced sterilizations," CNN.com, 17 November 2011. http://www. cnn.com/2011/11/17/world/americas/peru-sterilizations/?hpt=wo_t3

176 Paul Lombardo, "Eugenic Sterilization Laws," Image Archives on the American Eugenics Movement. http://www.eugenicsarchive. org/html/eugenics/essay8text.html

177 Interview with Elaine Riddick on *Maafa 21*, available at maafa21. com

178 Amnesty International USA, "Women in Indonesia & East Timor: Standing Against Repression," December 13, 1995, 15-16, 23. Cited in Mary Meehan, "How Eugenics and Population Control Led to Abortion," MeehanReports.com. http://www. meehanreports.com/how-led.html

179 Elizabeth Liagin, "East Africa: The Truth about Foreign Aid," Information Project for Africa newsletter, March 2000, 2, 4 & 1. Quoted in Mary Meehan, "How Eugenics and Population Control Led to Abortion," MeehanReports.com. http://www. meehanreports.com/how-led.html

180 Liu Yin (pseud.), "China's Wanted Children," *The Independent* (London), 11 Sept. 1991. Cited in Quoted in Mary Meehan, "How Eugenics and Population Control Led to Abortion," MeehanReports.com. http://www.meehanreports.com/how-led. html

181   This summary of Kinsey's research is taken from David Kupelian, *The Marketing of Evil* (Nashville: Cumberland House Publishing, 2005) 133.

182   Caleb Crain, "Alfred Kinsey: Liberator or Pervert?" NewYorkTimes.com, October 3, 2004 http://www.nytimes.com/2004/10/03/movies/03crai.html?pagewanted=print&position=&_r=0

183   Judith A. Reisman, "Crafting Bi/Homosexual Youth," *Regent University Law Review*, Vol. 14:283, p. 313. http://www.drjudithreisman.com/archives/regent.pdf

184   Christopher Turner, "Hugh Hefner in six volumes," *The Guardian*, 16 July 2010. http://www.guardian.co.uk/books/2010/jul/17/hugh-hefner-playboy-biography

185   Hollie McKay, "Hugh Hefner: Obama Should 'Get Out of the Wars,' FDR Was Best President," FoxNews.com, 2 August 2010. www.foxnews.com/entertainment/2010/08/02/hugh-hefner-obama-wars-fdr-best-president/#ixzz2LGca0glK

186   Carrie A. Pitzulo, *Bachelors and Bunnies: "Playboy" Magazine and Modern Heterosexuality, 1953—1973* (Chicago: University of Chicago Press, 2011) 225-30.

187   Ibid.

188   "Social Indicators of Marital health and Well-Being: trends of the Past Five Decades," National Marriage Project, University of Virginia, Figure 5. http://www.stateofourunions.org/2011/social_indicators.php#divorce

189   Albert Mohler, "No-Fault Divorce–The End of Marriage?" AlbertMohler.com, 7 March 2005. http://www.albertmohler.com/2005/03/07/no-fault-divorce-the-end-of-marriage-4/

190   "Social Indicators of Marital health and Well-Being: trends of the Past Five Decades," National Marriage Project, University of Virginia, Figure 8. http://www.stateofourunions.org/2011/social_indicators.php#cohabitation

191 "Number of sexual partners in lifetime," National Survey of Family Growth, Centers for Disease Control, http://www.cdc.gov/nchs/nsfg/abc_list_n.htm#numberlifetime

192 "Unmarried Childbearing," Fastats, Centers for Disease Control. http://www.cdc.gov/nchs/fastats/unmarry.htm

193 CDC Fact Sheet, "Incidence, Prevalence, and Cost of Sexually Transmitted Infections in the United States," Centers for Disease Control. http://www.cdc.gov/std/stats/STI-Estimates-Fact-Sheet-Feb-2013.pdf

194 Catharine A. MacKinnon, *Feminism Unmodified: Discourses on Life and Law* (President and Fellows of Harvard College, 1987) 99.

195 Ibid.

196 George Weigel, "The Libertine Police State," NationalReview.com, 13 February 2012. http://www.nationalreview.com/articles/290842/libertine-police-state-george-weigel

197 Dorchen Leidholdt, introduction, *The Sexual Liberals and the Attack on Feminism* (Pergamon Press, 1990) xv, footnote 8. Cited in Rene Denfeld, *The New Victorians: A Young Woman's Challenge to the Old Feminist Order* (New York: Warner Books, 1996), 55.

198 Mehdi Hasan, "Being pro-life doesn't make me any less of a lefty," NewStatesman.com, 11 October 2012. http://www.newstatesman.com/lifestyle/lifestyle/2012/10/being-pro-life-doesnt-make-me-any-less-lefty

199 Dr. John Cowan, *The Science of a New Life* (New York: Cowan and Company, 1871) 275. Cited in Olasky, *Abortion Rites*, 43.

200 John W. Trader, M.D., "Criminal Abortion," paper read before the Central Missouri Medical Association, Sedalia, MO, 6 October 1874, Toner Collection, Library of Congress. Cited in Olasky, *Abortion Rites*, 43.

201 Susan B. Anthony. *The Revolution*, 8 July 1869.

202 "Forced Abortion in America: A Special Report," The Elliot Institute. http://www.theunchoice.com/pdf/FactSheets/ForcedAbortions.pdf

203   Vincent M. Rue, Priscilla K. Coleman, James J. Rue, David C. Reardon, "Induced abortion and traumatic stress: A preliminary comparison of American and Russian women," *Medical Science Monitor*, 10(10): SR5-16. http://www.vozvictimas.org/pdf/documentos/rue2004.pdf

204   "Forced Abortion in America: A Special Report," The Elliot Institute. http://www.theunchoice.com/pdf/FactSheets/ForcedAbortions.pdf

205   Rue, et al., "Induced abortion and traumatic stress." http://www.vozvictimas.org/pdf/documentos/rue2004.pdf

206   Vincent M. Rue, Priscilla K. Coleman, James J. Rue, David C. Reardon, "Induced abortion and traumatic stress: A preliminary comparison of American and Russian women," *Medical Science Monitor*, 10(10): SR5-16. http://www.vozvictimas.org/pdf/documentos/rue2004.pdf

207   Abortion and Depression Part 1, Interview With Theresa Burke of Rachel's Vineyard Ministries, A Zenit Daily Dispatch, 4 March 2006. http://www.ewtn.com/library/PROLIFE/zabortdepr.htm

208   M Gissler et. al., "Pregnancy Associated Deaths in Finland 1987-1994 — definition problems and benefits of record linkage," *Acta Obsetricia et Gynecologica Scandinavica* 76:651-657 (1997).

209   DC Reardon et. al., "Deaths Associated With Pregnancy Outcome: A Record Linkage Study of Low Income Women," *Southern Medical Journal* 95(8):834-41, (2002). Cited in "Forced Abortion in America: A Special Report," The Elliot Institute.

210   M Gissler et. al., "Pregnancy Associated Deaths in Finland 1987-1994 — definition problems and benefits of record linkage," *Acta Obsetricia et Gynecologica Scandinavica* 76:651-657 (1997); and M. Gissler, "Injury deaths, suicides and homicides associated with pregnancy, Finland 1987-2000," *European J. Public Health* 15(5):459-63 (2005). Cited in "Forced Abortion in America: A Special Report," The Elliot Institute.

211   Vincent M. Rue, Priscilla K. Coleman, James J. Rue, David C. Reardon, "Induced abortion and traumatic stress: A preliminary

comparison of American and Russian women," *Medical Science Monitor*, 10(10): SR5-16. http://www.vozvictimas.org/pdf/documentos/rue2004.pdf. Cited in "Forced Abortion in America: A Special Report," The Elliot Institute.

212   Vincent M. Rue, Priscilla K. Coleman, James J. Rue, David C. Reardon, "Induced abortion and traumatic stress: A preliminary comparison of American and Russian women," *Medical Science Monitor*, 10(10): SR5-16. http://www.vozvictimas.org/pdf/documentos/rue2004.pdf. Cited in "Forced Abortion in America: A Special Report," The Elliot Institute.

213   Vincent M. Rue, Priscilla K. Coleman, James J. Rue, David C. Reardon, "Induced abortion and traumatic stress: A preliminary comparison of American and Russian women," *Medical Science Monitor*, ; 10(10): SR5-16. http://www.vozvictimas.org/pdf/documentos/rue2004.pdf. Cited in "Forced Abortion in America: A Special Report," The Elliot Institute.

214   See David C. Reardon, Ph.D., "Abortion Decisions and the Duty to Screen: Clinical, Ethical, and Legal Implications of Predictive Risk Factors of Post-Abortion Maladjustment," Manuscript based in part on an unpublished paper originally presented at the American Psychiatric Association Annual Meeting May 17-22, 1997, San Diego, CA. www.afterabortion.org/news/Duty2Screen.pdf

215   See www.theunchoice.com for further information and cases.

216   I.L. Horton and D. Cheng, "Enhanced Surveillance for Pregnancy-Associated Mortality-Maryland, 1993-1998," *JAMA* 285(11): 1455-1459 (2001); see also J. Mcfarlane et. al., "Abuse During Pregnancy and Femicide: Urgent Implications for Women's Health," Obstetrics & Gynecology 100: 27-36 (2002). Cited in "Forced Abortion in America: A Special Report," The Elliot Institute.

217   From "Forced Abortion in America: A Special Report," The Elliot Institute.

218 Kimport K, Foster K, Weitz TA, "Social sources of women's emotional difficulty after abortion: lessons from women's abortion narratives," *Perspectives on Sexual and Reproductive Health*, 2011 June; 43(2):103-9. http://www.ncbi.nlm.nih.gov/pubmed/21651709

219 Wanda Franz, Ph.D., "New Study Examines Familial Context of Choice to Abort," National Right to Life Committee. February 15, 2009. http://www.nrlc.org/News_and_Views/Jan09/nv011509.html

220 Priscilla K. Coleman, Charles David Maxey, Maria Spence, Charisse L. Nixon, "Predictors and Correlates of Abortion in the Fragile Families and Well-Being Study: Paternal Behavior, Substance Use, and Partner Violence," *International Journal of Mental Health and Addiction*, July 2009, Volume 7, Issue 3, pp. 405-22.

221 Vincent M. Rue, Ph.D., "'The Hollow Men': Male Grief & Trauma Following Abortion," United States Conference of Catholic Bishops, Washington, D.C. http://old.usccb.org/prolife/programs/rlp/rue.pdf

222 Kate Pickert, "What Choice?" *Time*, 14 Jan. 2013. http://www.time.com/time/magazine/article/0,9171,2132761,00.html#ixzz2LO2njBQy

223 "Use of Contraception in the United States: 1982–2008," Centers for Disease Control, Vital and Health Statistics, Series 23, Number 29, August 2010. http://www.cdc.gov/nchs/data/series/sr_23/sr23_029.pdf

224 U.S. Department of Health and Human Services. Use of Contraception in the United States: 1982-2008. (Centers for Disease Control and Prevention. National Center for Health Statistics) 15. http://www.cdc.gov/nchs/data/series/sr_23/sr23_029.pdf,

225 Finer LB and Zola MR, "Unintended pregnancy in the United States: incidence and disparities, 2006," *Contraception*, November

2011, Volume 84, Issue 5, 478-85. http://www.guttmacher.org/pubs/journals/j.contraception.2011.07.13.pdf

226   Finer LB et al., "Reasons U.S. women have abortions: quantitative and qualitative perspectives," *Perspectives on Sexual and Reproductive Health*, 2005, 37(3):110–8. Cited in "Facts on Induced Abortion in the United States August 2011," Guttmacher Institute. http://www.guttmacher.org/pubs/fb_induced_abortion.html

227   "Abortion: A Civilised Debate," http://www.youtube.com/watch?v=gLJK88QObrI

228   Bernard Nathanson, *The Hand of God* (Washington, D.C.: Regnery Gateway, 1996) 89-90.

229   *The Abortion Problem* (The Williams & Wilkins Co., 1944, publishing the proceedings of a 1942 conference) 28.

230   Christopher Tietze and Sarah Lewit, "Abortion," *Scientific America*, January 1969, Volume 220, 23. Cited in "What About Illegal Abortions?" Abort73.com, last updated June 20, 2012. http://www.abort73.com/end_abortion/what_about_illegal_abortions/

231   Mary Steichen Calderone, "Illegal Abortion As a Public Health Problem," *American Journal of Public Health*, July 1960, Vol. 50, Nol. 7, p. 949. http://www.ncbi.nlm.nih.gov/pmc/articles/PMC1373382/pdf/amjphnation00308-0022.pdf

232   Ibid.

233   "Abortion Surveillance — United States, 2003," Centers for Disease Control, 24 November 2006. http://www.cdc.gov/mmwr/preview/mmwrhtml/ss5511a1.htm

234   "List of motor vehicle deaths in U.S. by year," http://en.wikipedia.org/wiki/List_of_motor_vehicle_deaths_in_U.S._by_year

235   "Abortion Surveillance — United States, 2009 Surveillance Summaries," Morbidity and Mortality Weekly Report (MMWR), Centers for Disease Control, 23 November 2012, http://www.cdc.gov/mmwr/preview/mmwrhtml/ss6108a1.htm?s_cid=ss6108a1_w

236   Steven Ertelt, "Autopsy Proves Planned Parenthood Killed Woman in Botched Abortion," LifeNews.com, 11 September 2012.

http://www.lifenews.com/2012/09/11/autopsy-proves-planned-parenthood-killed-woman-in-botched-abortion/

237 "Carhart Patient Dead From Horrific 33-Week Abortion Injuries," OperationRescue.org, 8 February 2013. http://www.operationrescue.org/archives/carhart-patient-dead-from-horrific-33-week-abortion-injuries/

238 Maryclaire Dale, "Dr. Kermit Gosnell's Abortion Clinic: Women Say Abortions Left Them Sterile, Near Death," HuffingtonPost.com, 23 January 2011. http://www.huffingtonpost.com/2011/01/23/dr-kemit-gosnells-abortion-clinic_n_812701.html

239 Steven Ertelt, "Kermit Gosnell Drugged, Tied Up Woman Before Forced Abortion," LifeNews.com, 24 January 2011. http://www.lifenews.com/2011/01/24/kermit-gosnell-drugged-tied-up-woman-before-forced-abortion/

240 "New lawsuit: Planned Parenthood forced, botched abortion," Alliance Defending Freedom, 20 February 2013. http://www.adfmedia.org/News/PRDetail/7995

241 Ken Kolker, "Woman: Botched abortion nearly killed me," WOODTV.com, Tuesday, February 19, 2013 http://www.woodtv.com/dpp/news/target_8/WomanBotched-abortion-nearly-killed-me

242 Marc Thompson, "Photos show abortion clinic violations," WoodTV.com, January 7, 2013. http://www.woodtv.com/news/local/muskegon-county/photos-show-muskegon-abortion-clinic-code-violations

243 Mark Crutcher, *Lime 5* (Denton, Texas: Life Dynamics, Inc., 1996) 208-9.

244 "Physical Risks: Life-Threatening Risks of Abortion," Elliot Institute, http://www.theunchoice.com/pdf/FactSheets/PhysicalRisks.pdf

245 Dolle JM, Daling JR, White E, Brinton LA, Doody DR, Porter PL, and Malone KE. "Risk factors for triple-negative breast cancer in women under the age of 45 years," *Cancer Epidemiology,*

Biomarkers and Prevention 18, no. 4 (2009): 1157-66. Cited by Dr. Angela Lanfranchi in "Abortion as a Cause of Breast Cancer," presentation at National Press Club, 4 December 2012. http://www.slideshare.net/tjfjustice/lan-franci

246 See "Epidemiologic Studies: Induced Abortion and Breast Cancer Risk, Updated September 2012," Breast Cancer Prevention Institute, http://www.bcpinstitute.org/FactSheets/BCPI-FactSheet-Epidemiol-studies.pdf

247 Dr. Angela Lanfranchi in "Abortion as a Cause of Breast Cancer," presentation at National Press Club, 4 December 2012.

248 "What Has 40 Years of Abortion Done to America? Medical Aspects of Abortion on Women's Health," Abortion Media Summit presentation by Freda McKissic Bush, MD, FACOG at National Press Club, Washington, DC, 4 December 2012.

249 Swingle, HM, et al, "Abortion and the Risk of Subsequent Preterm Birth: A Systemic Review with Metanalysis," *Journal of Reproductive Medicine*, 54, 95-108 (2009). Cited in "What Has 40 Years of Abortion Done to America?
Medical Aspects of Abortion on Women's Health," Abortion Media Summit presentation by Freda McKissic Bush, MD, FACOG at National Press Club, Washington, DC, 4 December 2012.

250 "Study finds increased risk of prematurity and low birth weight in babies born after three or more abortions," 30 August 2012. http://www.eshre.eu/ESHRE/English/Press-Room/Press-Releases/Press-releases-2012/Babies-born-after-three-or-more-abortions/page.aspx/1675

251 Larry Lader, "The Abortion Revolution," *The Humanist*, May/June 1973, 4. Cited in "Impact of Abortion on Society," Life.org.nz. http://www.life.org.nz/abortion/abortionkeyissues/impact-on-society-abortion/Default.htm

252 Patricia Coleman, et al., "Associations between voluntary and involuntary forms of perinatal loss and child maltreatment among

low-income mothers," *Acta Paediatrica*. 2005 Oct; 94(10): 1476-83. http://www.ncbi.nlm.nih.gov/pubmed/16299880

253 Michael J. New, "Abortion Promises Unfulfilled," *The Public Discourse*, The Witherspoon Institute, 23 January 2013. http://www.thepublicdiscourse.com/2013/01/7630/

254 Crystal Phend, "Child-Abuse Injuries on the Rise," ABCNews.go.com, 1 October 2012. http://abcnews.go.com/Health/Wellness/child-abuse-injuries-rise/story?id=17364578

255 John and Barbara Willke, *Abortion: Questions and Answers* (Cincinnati, Ohio: Hayes Publishing Company, 2003), 283.

256 Philip G. Ney, M.D. "Abortion and Child Abuse: Which is Cause, Which is Effect?" David Mall and Walter F. Watts, M.D. (Editors). Proceedings of the conference "Psychological Aspects of Abortion." Sponsored on October 31 and November 1, 1978, by the Stritch School of Medicine, Loyola University, Chicago, Illinois. Published by University Publications of America. Quoted in Dr. Brian Clowes, *Pro-Life Encyclopedia*, Chapter 41 (American Life League, 1995). http://www.ewtn.com/library/PROLENC/ENCYC041.HTM

257 Philip G. Ney, M.D. "Clinician's View: Relationship Between Abortion and Child Abuse." *Canadian Journal of Psychiatry*, July 1979, pages 610 to 620. Quoted in Dr. Brian Clowes, *Pro-Life Encyclopedia*, Chapter 41 (American Life League, 1995). http://www.ewtn.com/library/PROLENC/ENCYC041.HTM

258 Erica Jong, "If Men Could Get Pregnant, Abortion Would be a Sacrament," HuffingtonPost.com, 21 January 2008. http://www.huffingtonpost.com/erica-jong/if-men-could-get-pregnant_b_82467.html

259 "Abortion Risks: A list of major physical complications related to abortion," http://afterabortion.org/1999/abortion-risks-a-list-of-major-physical-complications-related-to-abortion/

260 Ibid.

261 "Abortion Four Times Deadlier Than Childbirth," Elliot Institute, 3 June 2000. http://afterabortion.org/2000/abortion-four-times-deadlier-than-childbirth/

262 Priscilla K. Coleman, "Abortion and mental health: quantitative synthesis and analysis of research published 1995–2009," *British Journal of Psychiatry*, (2011) 199: 180-6. http://bjp.rcpsych.org/content/199/3/180.abstract

263 "Huge 2011 study: Abortion and mental health: quantitative synthesis and analysis of research published 1995-2009," American Association of Pro-Life Obstetricians and Gynecologists. http://www.aaplog.org/complications-of-induced-abortion/induced-abortion-and-mental-health/huge-new-study-abortion-and-mental-health-quantitative-synthesis-and-analysis-of-research-published-1995-2009/

264 "Abortion and Substance Abuse Link Often Overlooked, Women's Health Review Reports," Elliot Institute, 20 January 2005. http://afterabortion.org/2005/abortion-and-substance-abuse-link-often-overlooked-womens-health-review-reports/

265 "Risk of Psychiatric Hospitalization Rises After Abortion," Elliot Institute, 22 September 2003. http://afterabortion.org/2003/risk-of-psychiatric-hospitalization-rises-after-abortion/

266 Dr. Bryan C. Calhoun, "40 Years of Abortion," see slide 12 of PowerPoint presentation. http://www.40yearsafterabortion.org/dr-byron-c-calhoun-md/

267 Philip G. Ney, MD, "Siblings of People Dying in Abortions Suffer Depression," LifeNews.com, 27 July 2011. http://www.lifenews.com/2011/07/27/siblings-of-people-dying-in-abortions-suffer-depression/

268 Anita H. Weiner, Eugene C. Weiner, "The aborted sibling factor: A case study," *Clinical Social Work Journal*, Fall 1984, Volume 12, Issue 3, pages 209-215. http://link.springer.com/article/10.1007%2FBF00759918?LI=true

269 Catherine T. Coyle, "Men and Abortion: A Review of Empirical Reports Concerning the Impact of Abortion on Men," *The Internet*

Journal of Mental Health, 2007 Volume 3 Number 2. DOI: 10.5580/290. http://www.ispub.com/journal/the-internet-journal-of-mental-health/volume-3-number-2/men-and-abortion-a-review-of-empirical-reports-concerning-the-impact-of-abortion-on-men. html#sthash.LQfDk8ss.SwgGPsXE.dpuf

270 Ibid.

271 Catherine T. Coyle, RN, PhD, "Men and Abortion: Psychological Effects," http://www.menandabortion.net/MAN/pdf/men_abortion_summary_table.pdf

272 "A Father's Testimony: I was a coward," Priestsforlife.org. http://www.priestsforlife.org/postabortion/casestudyproject/casestudy760.htm

273 "Reflection from a father," Priestsforlife.org. http://www.priestsforlife.org/testimonies/document-print.aspx?ID=2692

274 Account relayed personally to the author.

275 Vincent M. Rue, Ph.D., "'The Hollow Men': Male Grief & Trauma Following Abortion," U.S. Conference of Catholic Bishops, 2008. http://old.usccb.org/prolife/programs/rlp/rue.pdf

276 Ibid.

277 "The internet porn 'epidemic': By the numbers," TheWeek.com, 17 June 2010. http://theweek.com/article/index/204156/the-internet-porn-epidemic-by-the-numbers

278 Statement on abortion from the Book of Discipline of The United Methodist Church. http://www.umc.org/site/apps/nlnet/content.aspx?c=lwL4KnN1LtH&b=5066287&ct=6467539

279 Marvin Olasky, *Telling the Truth: How to Revitalize Christian Journalism.* http://www.worldmag.com/world/olasky/truth12.html

280 Frederica Mathewes-Green, "How should churches handle the delicate issue of abortion when nearly one-fifth of women who get abortions are sitting in our pews?" ChristianityToday.com, 18 January 2011. http://www.christianitytoday.com/biblestudies/bible-answers/spirituallife/sittingourpews.html?start=1

281 Rachel K. Jones, Lawrence B. Finer and Susheela Singh, "Characteristics of U.S. Abortion Patients, 2008," Guttmacher Institute, 9-10. http://www.guttmacher.org/pubs/US-Abortion-Patients.pdf

282 "Estimated Median Age at First Marriage, by Sex: 1890 to the Present," U.S. Census Bureau. http://www.census.gov/hhes/families/files/ms2.csv

283 Robin Marantz Henig, "Why are so many people in their 20s taking so long to grow up?" *New York Times*, 18 August 2010. http://www.nytimes.com/2010/08/22/magazine/22Adulthood-t.html?_r=0

284 "Young Men and Women Differ on the Importance of a Successful Marriage," Pew Research Center, 26 April 2012. http://www.pewresearch.org/daily-number/young-men-and-women-differ-on-the-importance-of-a-successful-marriage/

285 Hannah Rosin, "The End of Men," TheAtlantic.com, July/August 2010. http://www.theatlantic.com/magazine/archive/2010/07/the-end-of-men/308135/

286 S. T. Karnick, "Girly Men: The Media's Attack on Masculinity," Salvo.org. http://www.salvomag.com/new/articles/salvo4/4karnick.php

287 "The Feminization of the American male," RedState.com. http://archive.redstate.com/blogs/bs/2008/jun/13/the_feminization_of_the_american_male

288 Dr. Laura Schlessinger, *The Proper Care and Feeding of Marriage* (New York: HarperCollins Publisher, 2007) 3.

289 Spectrum, National Public Radio, May 11, 1990. Cited in Mark Crutcher, *Lime 5: Exploited by Choice* (Denton, Texas: Life Dynamics, Incorporated, 1996) 175-6.

290 Thaddeus M. Baklinski, "Researcher: Economic Impact of Abortion in U.S. Since 1970 - $35 to $70 Trillion," LifeSiteNews.com, 21 October 2008. http://www.lifesitenews.com/news/archive//ldn/2008/oct/08102109

291   Patrick F. Fagan, Ph.D., "The Effects of Pornography on
        Individuals, Marriage, Family, and Community," Marriage and
        Religion Research Institute, December 2009.

292   CDC Fact Sheet: Incidence, Prevalence, and Cost of Sexually
        Transmitted Infections in the United States. http://www.cdc.gov/
        std/stats/STI-Estimates-Fact-Sheet-Feb-2013.pdf

293   "Why Abstinence?" Medical Institute for Sexual Health. https://
        www.medinstitute.org/2012/08/why-abstinence/

294   Stephen Davis, *Walk This Way: The Autobiography of Aerosmith*
        (Dogeared Publishing, reprint edition, 2003) 275.

295   Steven Ertelt, "Unreleased Michael Jackson "Pro-Life" Song
        "Abortion Papers" Now Out," LifeNews.com, 24 September 2012.
        http://www.lifenews.com/2012/09/24/unreleased-michael-jackson-
        pro-life-song-abortion-papers-now-out/#sthash.wWYbsqIB.dpuf

296   David Bereit, Shawn Carney, *40 Days for Life: Discover What God
        Has Done ... Imagine What He Can Do* (Cappella Books, Kindle
        Edition, 2013), Kindle Locations 1917-21.

297   Frances Moore Lappe, "Beyond the scarcity scare: reframing the
        discourse of hunger with an eco-mind,"
        The Journal of Peasant Studies, Vol. 40, No. 1, 219–238, page 221.
        ["The world food supply comes to about 2800 calories each day for
        every person on Earth, enough to make us all chubby (FAOSTAT
        2011b)."] http://www.tandfonline.com/doi/pdf/10.1080/0306615
        0.2012.708859

298   Dr. Catherine T. Coyle, "Men and Abortion: Finding Healing,
        Restoring Hope," Knights of Columbus Supreme Council, 26.
        http://www.kofc.org/un/en/resources/cis/cis334.pdf

299   David Bereit, Shawn Carney, *40 Days for Life: Discover What God
        Has Done ... Imagine What He Can Do* (Cappella Books, Kindle
        Edition, 2013) Kindle Locations 389-92.

300   Ibid., Kindle Locations 410-3.

INDEX